Word Power Makes the Difference

Making What You Write Pay Off

Duane Newcomb

Parker Publishing Co., Inc.
West Nyack, New York

Library of Congress Cataloging in Publication Data

Newcomb, Duane G
  Word power makes the difference.

  1. English language--Composition and exercises.
2. Communication. I. Title.
PE1408.N44   808'.042   74-23393
ISBN 0-13-963371-5

Printed in the United States of America

Other Works by the Author

Spare-Time Fortune Guide
The Wonderful World of Houseboating

What This Book Can Do for You

Bad writing—really bad writing—costs businesses and individuals millions of dollars every year.

It wastes the time and energy of everyone who tries to understand it, produces thousands of mistakes, destroys tons of paper, takes up hundreds of hours of writing time, and, in the end, produces practically no results.

Several years ago, communications pioneers (among them Rudolph Flesch and Robert Gunning) turned the writing world upside down and taught all of us how to communicate more effectively . . . yet, while they showed us how to write so our readers could understand us easily, they stopped far short of doing the entire job.

To get the most out of every piece of writing you have to do more. An interoffice memo, for instance, might tell another employee that you want him to go to his files and send you two copies of Company Y's contract. He knows exactly what you want, yet does nothing. *Why?* Because effective written communication is only half the battle. To get action, *real action,* you must not only communicate, but motivate.

And that's what this book, *Word Power Makes the Difference,* is all about. It combines the science of effective communication with motivational psychology. It includes such elements as speaking in terms of reader needs, crashing through your reader's boredom barrier to shake him wide awake, and more.

Currently many large companies spend millions every year trying to teach their executives to write effectively, but never before have they been welded into an effective system that breaks the principles down into basic components and makes them an effective *communication-action* tool.

That is exactly what this book does.

The first section shows you how to make words work for you: how to make your writing come alive—how to get rid of sludge—how to put it in plain-talk—and more.

The next section of the book gives you the basic impact tools: how to reach up from a piece of paper and grab your reader—how to make your writing more exciting—how to make goals work for you—how to put your ideas in power packed order—and more.

Chapters 8, 9, 10, and 11 are the motivational chapters; they show you: how to get through to your reader by turning words into pictures—how to move people by producing emotion—how to motivate by thinking in terms of reader needs—how and when to be outrageous.

Finally, the last chapter shows you exactly how to take all the word power tools and utilize them in every type of writing to really produce results.

Duane Newcomb

Contents

What This Book Can Do for You 5

1. How to Make Word Power Work for You 9

How to Achieve Word Impact ● The Basic Word Power Formula

2. How to Cash in on the Power of Plain Talk 19

Check It with a Readability Index ● Keep Sentence Length in Check ● Come to the Point Immediately ● Just Tell Your Reader About It ● Keep the Essentials and Make It Simple in Between ● Grammar Doesn't Count ● Take Out All Unnecessary Words ● In Conclusion

3. How to Write for Word Power Impact 37

Utilize Active Verbs ● Make It Come Alive ● Utilize One Thought Per Sentence ● Arrange Your Thoughts in Build-Up Order ● Wind Up with a Bang

4. How to Unsludge Your Writing 49

5. How to Command Attention on Paper 61

How to Grab Readers with a Ho-Hum Breaker ● Tell Your Reader What to Expect ● Use Reader Guideposts to Command Attention ● Ask a Question—Then Answer It ● Use Novelty to Carry Readers ● Make It off-the-Cuff ● Use Short Staccato Sentences for Effect ● How It Looks Makes a Difference ● How to Make It More Exciting

6. Developing the Word Power of Goal Direction 81

Make Every Piece of Writing Have a Purpose ● How to Decide on a Purpose ● How to Organize for Goal Achievement ● Make Each Paragraph Lead in a Goal Direction ● Three Steps to Written Goal Achievement

7. **Putting Your Ideas in Power Packed Order** 93

How to Organize for Impact ● How to Increase the Impact ● How to Utilize an Impact Formula ● In Conclusion

8. **How to Use a Word Image Projector** 111

How to Use Picture Words for Impact ● How to Turn Ideas into Pictures ● How to Use Comparisons Effectively ● Don't Get Trapped by Collapsed Words ● How to Utilize Symbols for Impact ● How to Use Projected Pictures to Achieve Reader Understanding ● In Conclusion

9. **How to Make Emotion Work for You** 127

How to Put Emotion in Writing ● Subtle Emotion ● Emotional Word Guide ● How to Utilize an Emotional Goal ● How to Use Increased Word Excitement for Impact ● How to Appeal Emotionally to People ● How to Use Emotional Appeal to Make People Respond

10. **How to Motivate Through Word Power** 143

Future Promise ● How to Use the "I Factor" to Create Response ● Think in Terms of the Other Person's Needs ● In Conclusion ● Examples of Writing that Considers the Other Person's Needs and Utilizes Common Trait Appeal ● Intensive Researched Writing Directed to the Reader's Needs

11. **How to Make Brashness Pay Off** 159

12. **How to Apply Word Power to All Kinds of Writing** 171

How to Decide on the Elements You'll Need ● Letters ● Memos ● Pamphlets ● Reports ● In Conclusion

1

How
to Make Word Power
Work for You

Practically every one of us writes something every day. Most of us do it to get something done—to put an idea across to a subordinate— to report to the boss—to finish a school assignment—to impart some sort of message to someone for which we expect some kind of action.

And believe me, words *do* get action. Words can make a country go to war, get you a job, get you fired, get you a wife, and also a divorce. Words, under certain circumstances, create a powerful impact.

For instance, two years ago, Bill Jones, a young Californian just out of college, was faced with a problem. He seriously wanted a job with a well-known company, but knew that since he had far less sales experience than most of the other 1000 prospects who would apply, his chances of getting an interview, much less the job itself, were slim. He thought about this for a while, then sent the company a short letter which ended: *"In addition to the above qualifications, I have a simple idea which should make your company an additional million dollars in sales every year."*

Needless to say, he was one of the final 20 called for an interview. After the interview, although the company didn't use his idea, it hired Bill on the basis of other qualifications. Later he became his company's star salesman. "If you hadn't added that final sentence," the interviewer later told Bill, "you would never have been called in."

In another case, Leonard Martin, a 39 year old electric product company employee who had been five years on the job without a raise, had come up with an idea for packaging one of the company's trouble light products. He was sure his idea would raise sales. Unfortunately, several notes to his immediate superior failed to bring any response, and his requests to talk to the company president were all turned down.

Leonard thought about this for some time, then sat down and wrote a note which simply said:

Good morning, Mr. Rizzo:

I want to suggest an idea that I'm certain will double sales of the 101 trouble light.

It's too detailed to describe in a letter, but if I could talk to you in person, I could give you details.

Leonard mailed the letter Monday morning, at 11:00 AM. Tuesday, he was in the boss' office talking about the idea.

It was as good an idea as he had said, and within a month Leonard was in charge of carrying out the project. During the next two years he came up with two other ideas which did equally well, and at the end of that time was made products manager. None of this, of course, would have occurred if Leonard had not written the note which caught his boss' attention and made him respond.

And in still another case, Janet Rutledge, a San Francisco housewife, was trying to get her washing machine's pump fixed. The dealer had ignored her phone calls until the warranty expired and two phone calls to the company's district representative brought no results. Finally she sat down and jotted a note to the company president.

It started: *Is your company's reputation worth $20?*

She then continued, explaining briefly that she had used their products many years and had had great faith in them. Now, however, a $20 repair was completely destroying her confidence, and would destroy that of all other customers if they were being treated the same way.

She then went on to say she hated to see the company ruin a reputation that had taken years to build.

Finally, she ended by stating she felt that $20 was a small price to pay for a reputation and she hoped the company felt the same way.

Within three days, the company president phoned. He agreed that the company was indeed dependent on its reputation and wouldn't be in business very long without it. Two weeks later she received a brand new washing machine and another letter thanking her for her thoughts—another example of words that get *positive action.*

HOW TO ACHIEVE WORD IMPACT

Writing too often simply "sits" on the printed page and does nothing. This is because there is a tremendous difference between the potential impact words have and the actual impact they create in a piece of writing.

How many times, for instance, have you received written instructions from another person which you had trouble understanding and which you finally stopped reading because you just couldn't sustain interest? In addition, how many times have you written a letter expecting immediate action and received almost no response? The fact is that written communication often falls flat.

There is, however, no reason for this, for words have tremendous potential. However, to make them achieve this potential *you must communicate clearly, immediately get the reader's attention,* and *motivate him to action once he reads what is written.*

This combination of verbal elements used to achieve word impact we call WORD POWER. Word power always has an effect on your reader and produces a far greater action (as a result of a written message) than any other method.

This book then will help you achieve word power mastery and increase the effectiveness of your writing many times. Each chapter will add a new tool.

The remainder of this chapter will give you a simple formula which will let you start utilizing the word power principles immediately.

THE BASIC WORD POWER FORMULA

The basic word power formula consists primarily of three

things: *keep it simple, get your reader's attention,* and *talk directly to your reader.* There are many facets to each of these which we will take up later, but you don't need all the details to get started. All you need now is to be aware that each is important, and to try to include some or all of these elements in everything you write.

Keep It Simple

This is a basic rule that should be applied at all times. One of the main problems is that people often use too many words to say what they're trying to say, and the writing itself is too complicated. You can, however, greatly improve your writing if you look at everything you write and ask: Is this the simplest way I can say it and still include everything I want to say? If it isn't, rewrite it.

For instance, if you write: *My various efforts at organizing my thoughts have finally gotten me to the point where I'm now ready to write this letter,* you're doing a terrible job. That sentence isn't simple and straightforward, so apply the basic rule and try to make it as simple as possible without changing the meaning. Once you do that it becomes: *I'm now ready to write this letter.*

Try this yourself with these sentences. Place a sheet of paper over the simple forms on the right side and try to simplify these complicated statements on a separate sheet of paper.

Complicated	Simple
We would be very happy if after thinking it over you would reply.	Please reply.
The first step we must take it appears to me is to get down to basics.	We must get down to basics.
We'll try to do the job now, next week, or by the end of the second week.	We'll try to do the job within the next two weeks.
The object of this form is to request your compliance with the rules.	We'd like you to comply with the rules.
I didn't mean to do it that way but since I couldn't think of any other way to do it, I did it that way.	I did it unintentionally.
I got the right address when my first letter was returned with another address which I see is correct.	I got the right address from the envelope when my first letter was returned.

Complicated	Simple
Because I have a lot of other things to do and they take a lot of time, I don't think I'll be able to go on the trip.	I don't think I can go on the trip because I have a lot of time-consuming things to do.
I didn't get your letter because I wasn't here when the postman brought it the first time and he took it back.	I wasn't here when the postman brought your letter so he took it back.
Continue to keep us in mind when you have anything in our area of concern.	Let us know when you have anything we might like.
Your suggestions will indeed be discussed during the next Publications Committee meeting.	We will discuss your suggestions at the next Publications Committee meeting.
When I'm standing in front of the bank and I look tired I'd appreciate it if you'd stop and give me a lift.	I'd like you to give me a lift whenever I'm standing in front of the bank and look tired.

Get Your Reader's Attention

Much writing simply starts without giving the reader any reason to read on. As a result, often the first couple of sentences get read then the writing's put down. To combat this tendency you should always do something at the beginning of each piece of writing to attract attention. There are many ways to do this, and they will be covered in detail in a future chapter. In the beginning, however, you can improve your writing tremendously if you remember that a reader will always read on if you offer him some future promise. How? By changing the sentence around so the reader feels you are offering him something he can use.

Let's see how this works. You write: *There are many ways to make money and some of them are easy to learn.* This isn't too bad, but it doesn't offer much promise. Let's see if we can't promise our reader a little more, like this: *You can learn to make money in many ways. Here are a few:*

Of course, "promise" is more effective when you appeal directly to the reader with the word "you." But you can also offer the promise of additional needed information or something similar in the third person.

Now see if you can do this by yourself: Place a piece of paper over the answers on the right-hand side and see if you can offer the reader some future promise that will make him want to read on.

Poor Beginnings	Attention Getting Beginnings
The high school carnival was a success and we got marvelous response in our call for donations and help for the Country Store ... and a lot of people helped in phoning and in putting in a lot of long hours ... thanks a lot.	Thank you very much for helping to make our School Carnival a tremendous success. This was due to ...
This summer at King Memorial Library we had a Creative Writer's Workshop.	Let me tell you about the Creative Writer's Workshop we had at King Memorial Library.
In order to eliminate the possibility of errors occurring ...	Here are several ways to eliminate errors.
Paris is lovely in the spring ...	I'd like to share Paris in the spring with you.
From prior contact with you, I am aware of your interest in real estate. Therefore I thought you would like to know of a land investment which I am offering.	Here's a land investment that might interest you. (Now you can tell him the rest.)
In many years in business we have learned that some customers like to be called on the phone before seeing the salesman in person. This often results in bigger orders.	Customers will often give you larger orders if you will call them before going in ... (now you can fill in the details.)
According to a report released today by the Federal Trade Commission, Drugs and Medicines lead the most profitable industry parade.	Drugs and Medicines are the most profitable industries ... (the reader will now read on to find out what you're talking about and who said so.)
Bill Thomas Corporation, maker of Thompson and Harnell outboard motors and related recreational products, today announced that 150 snowmobiles powered by newly developed OMC rotation combustion engines are being placed in the hands	The Bill Thomas Corporation will consumer field test 150 OMC rotation combustion engine powered snowmobiles to see how they operate. This will be handled by ... (now your readers will keep reading to get the details.)

Poor Beginnings	Attention Getting Beginnings
of selected dealers for a consumer field test.	
There's no benefit in going into a long-winded explanation about delays in payment. But the problems have been squared away and will not recur. What we're going to do is . . .	Here's what's going to happen about the payment delay.
Mr. Myers has asked that I answer your letter regarding a unit for a magazine article. I know from past experience. . .	Here's the answer to your request for a unit.

Talk Directly to Your Reader

You have already begun to do this by inserting the word "you." But you can also do this with the first person plural. For instance, you write: *This course thoroughly covers all the principles of good investment.* This doesn't appeal very much, so you add the "you" and write: *This course will teach you the principles of good investment.* That's better. However, to stay in the original tone and still add appeal you could write: *This course will teach all of us the principles of good investment.* Of course, not every type of writing will allow you to talk directly to your reader, but where you can, you'll increase your written effectiveness 100 percent or more. Now try your own hand at this. Place a piece of paper over the answers on the right-hand side, and try to insert a "you" in each of these.

Indirect	Talking to Your Reader
Students who want an A will do the examples at the end of the book.	If you want an A you will do the examples at the end of the book.
Those who use this method will find out how to lose five pounds easily.	Using this method you can easily lose five pounds.
Emotion in a piece of writing helps keep interest up.	You can keep interest up by inserting emotion in a piece of writing.
Special thanks to those people who helped us.	A special thank you for helping us.
It's possible to build a cabin using only the materials on the site.	You can build a cabin using only the materials on the site.
Many people learn to ski easily.	You can learn to ski easily *or* Many of us can learn to ski easily.

Indirect	Talking to Your Reader
Sometimes it's hard to get up in the morning.	You will sometimes find it hard to get up in the morning.
People can lose their jobs because the boss doesn't like them.	You can lose your job because the boss doesn't like you.
These stamps will have to be put on carefully.	You will have to put these stamps on carefully.
There are probably many people who would like girls chasing them.	Would you like girls chasing you?

There are many types of writing in which you can't talk to your reader. But when you can it will improve both the communication and response many times.

Word Power Dynamics, then, will teach you how to both communicate with other people and motivate them to action. And as you master each individual word power principle, you will discover that this method (presented for the first time in this book) will do more to improve your writing skills than anything else that you may have tried.

2

How
to Cash in on
the Power of Plain Talk

In some ways this might be called the Age of Writing. Nearly everyone is called upon to write something every day. The boss sends instructions to his salesmen, employees report on the day's activities in writing, the housewife jots notes to her children, and students write papers on every conceivable subject.

Yet, bad writing causes an almost incalculable amount of damage and trouble. Good writing, on the other hand, can pay off handsomely.

For instance, Ralph Miller, a factory foreman who couldn't understand the complex written rules and regulations on his income tax form, saved almost $500 by following six concise, written rules given him by a local C.P.A.

Bill White, a Spokane, Washington, bus driver, saved $400 by following precise written instructions on how to take the family at half-rate to a well-known resort.

Sam Grimes, a small machinery manufacturing company salesman, made the company $1000 because he communicated concisely in a written memo exactly how to receive an extra bonus by shipping immediately. And George Hendricks, a shipping clerk, received a special $300 reward from his company for the excellent written communication that his two man office turned out.

Actually clear, concise, easy-to-understand writing offers many advantages. The problem is that the more difficult you make a piece of writing, the less your reader will understand it. At first, he'll simply miss some of the points you're trying to make, but, finally, if you make it difficult enough he'll stop reading altogether.

Ever wonder why, for instance, you couldn't learn easily from a textbook? Chances are it wasn't because the subject was difficult, but because the author didn't explain the subject matter clearly. Recent tests have shown that students actually learn three or four times faster than they normally would when the text material is uncomplicated.

There are other benefits from clear, concise communications: mistakes decrease, readers can read the written material faster and retain more, and everyday life in general becomes simpler. As a result, plain talk actually has the power to save every one of us time, money, and energy in almost every activity that involves the written word.

Learning to communicate clearly only accounts for one-third of the word power tools that will make your writing produce action. Yet it is extremely important, for unless you can communicate clearly you will never be able to use the other word power tools effectively. In this chapter you will take up the Plain Talk side of clear communication, learning how to keep sentence length in check, how to come to the point immediately, how to write like you talk, and how to get rid of unnecessary words that diffuse meaning.

CHECK IT WITH A READABILITY INDEX

Just how do you know when you're writing plainly? You don't, not unless you have a guide, and there are some good ones available. But before I give you a readability guide to use in your own writing let's consider what people prefer to read.

Probably the most universally read magazine in the United States today is the *Reader's Digest.* Millions "devour" it every month and almost everyone can understand it easily. *Sports Illustrated, McCalls* and *Newsweek* are also read by an extremely large audience. They are a little more difficult to read than *Reader's Digest,* but certainly clear and understandable. But as we move toward the *Atlantic Monthly* and *Harper's Magazine* we begin to lose our audience. These last two are considered primarily "highbrow" magazines and almost all of their readers are both college-trained and intellectually inclined. Beyond this, we find technical writing, government information (but not all), textbooks, and similar material which very few readers will even try to read unless it's absolutely necessary.

Obviously then, to get through to your readers effectively, you should stay somewhere in the middle range of the *Reader's Digest, Sports Illustrated, McCalls, Newsweek*, and similar magazines. The question is, of course, just what is this middle range? There are a number of readability guides. The one developed by Rudolf Flesch, and Robert Gunning's *Fog Count* are probably two of the best, but I find both a little cumbersome to use, so I will outline one here which can be applied a little more easily to your writing.

(1) Count the number of sentences in a sample of 100 words and divide the number of sentences into 100. (This is the average number of words per sentence.) (2) Count all the words over seven letters in length. (3) Add both figures together and divide the sum by two. This gives you a workable readability index. For instance, a 100 word passage with six sentences and six words with over seven letters each adds up this way: 100/6 equals 16. 16 plus 6 equals 22. Divide this by 2, and you have a readability index of 11.

Here's how some well-known reading material tests out:

Children's writing	10–12
General magazines	13–15
Literary magazines	17–20
Most textbooks, technical materials	23 plus

For good readability then you should try to keep your own writing somewhere between a readability index of 12 to 16. Several studies have shown that employees that communicate best are those who get the better jobs and are promoted fastest. In addition, people who keep their writing in this range get more action, better understanding from others, and an overall favorable response.

KEEP SENTENCE LENGTH IN CHECK

People read in sentences, not in words. Research over the last 20 years to determine the effect of sentence length on readability has shown that the longer a sentence is, the harder it is to read.

Here is a gauge:

Very Easy	8 words or less per sentence
Easy	9–11 words
Fairly Easy	12–14 words
Average	15–19 words
Fairly Hard	20–24 words
Hard	25–28 words
Very Hard	29 words or more

This doesn't mean that every sentence you write should be 15 to 19 words long. That would be boring. Mix it up, have a few eight word sentences, some 25 word sentences, some 15–19 word sentences, and a few in between. Overall, however, make sure your sentences average in the "fairly easy" to "average" range.

Now try to gauge for yourself how easy a sentence is to read without paying too much attention to its actual length. Place a piece of paper over the right-hand side and rate each sentence as to whether it's average, very easy, easy, fairly easy, fairly hard, hard, or very hard:

Sentences	Degree of Difficulty
I think I'm going to cry.	easy
Although you haven't been with us very long, you can probably see by everything that goes on here that we are in deep trouble.	fairly difficult
It really looks like Johnny will be in trouble before he finishes this performance.	fairly easy
When a car hits yours head-on it drives you upon your steering wheel and column.	average
So the beginner who is not a beginner but something of a hot-shot back home on the packed down trails he is used to adjusts his goggles and his white-silk scarf, brings his right thumb and forefinger together gallantly and steels his nerve.	hard

Sentences	Degree of Difficulty
Rapid growth calls for rapid building.	easy
The "ghost town" is a distinctive American institution in which whole communities have packed up and moved on, thriving only in distant memory.	fairly hard
Robert had often experienced the tragedy of others.	easy
The older infant wants to manipulate objects such as cradle gyms he can pull on and swat at.	average
Last June, in the famous New York City's Bronx, the doors opened on the Lilia Acheson Wallace World of Birds.	average (count the name as one word unless extremely long)

COME TO THE POINT IMMEDIATELY

Can you imagine plowing through sentence after sentence without finding out what the point is? I won't do it and you probably won't, either. Yet, writers frequently run five, six, seven, and more paragraphs before they let their reader know about what they're talking. This is foolish. After all, it's extremely difficult to hold a person's attention anytime. In writing, it's doubly difficult because all that reader has to do is shift his eyes and he's gone.

For instance, Roger Billings, who owned a part-time mail order business, wrote two different direct mail pieces for a novelty pencil sharpener, each of which he mailed to 500 potential customers. In the first he talked about the benefits of a good pencil sharpener in a rambling way and didn't mention the sharpener itself until the fifth sentence. The second started out by simply saying: You can now buy an unusual novelty pencil sharpener. Then he went on to explain the other details. The second ad pulled three times as many responses as the first and made Roger well over $1800.

Because readers pay more attention when you come to the point immediately, it is vital to quickly tell your reader what you intend to say. If possible, do it in the first sentence. If that isn't practical, then try to state your point within the first paragraph. The rule is this: Decide what the reader wants to know and state that first, then fill in the remaining details in logical order.

Now, let's see if you can handle a few of these rambling beginnings. Look through the sentences on the left, (put a piece of paper over the answers on the right) and see if you can make those sentences readable.

The Rambling Way

The papers that won the poetry contest were marked with a big red X and put on the board at the front of the room; the rest were stacked in a neat pile at the back. There was a lot of talk about canceling, but several of the teachers talked to the principal and he finally decided not to. The poetry contest itself was held Saturday and about 200 people came. I think Bill James, Tom Jordan, and Mary Halverston finally won.

It is difficult to put the Easy Master table together unless you have the proper light. The box looks like it doesn't contain enough parts but it does. If you will follow instructions on page four it will go together easily.

An eminent person asked to itemize the qualities demanded by his own work or by any task which he supervises names every desirable trait, partly because every job he does requires all, but in different degrees. The only sound procedure, that of measuring persons of proved accomplishment and so determine empirically what differentiates them from others is not always possible.

The "Right" Way

(Decide what the reader wants to know, state that, then fill in the details in some order.) Bill James, Tom Jordan and Mary Halverston won last Saturday's poetry contest. The winning poems were displayed on the board at the front of the room, the rest were stacked in a neat pile at the back. At one time it was thought the contest might be canceled, but since 200 people came, the teachers talked to the principal, and it was allowed to continue.

To put your Easy Master table together, simply follow the instructions on page four. The Easy Master package contains all the parts you will need. For easy assembly, put it together in the proper light.

Only one or two traits are really necessary in handling any particular job or task. Most eminent people, however, list many desirable traits when asked to decide what qualities are demanded by their own work. Actually, the only sound way to do this—although not always possible—is to measure persons of proved accomplishment and determine how they differ from other people.

JUST TELL YOUR READER ABOUT IT

This is an extremely important rule. If you want to write plainly you can do so by talking to your reader as if he were sitting across from you. How you do it will probably depend on whom you're talking to, but it should be plain and easy to understand. That doesn't mean you must omit key elements. By all means, keep all necessary words, but if the final version doesn't sound like the way you'd talk to another person, then say it another way. After that, if you're still not satisfied it's really conversational and easy to understand, illustrate the point with some examples.

Now let's see if we can put a few of these principles into actual practice. Here's one: *The effective execution of every business and industrial task requires training during which a novice accepts in pay more than he produces.*

This isn't good communication. And if you expect most people to understand you, you've got to make it conversational like this: *It is necessary to have some training for almost every job and during the training period probably no beginning worker is really worth what he gets.*

What we really did was to connect up the basic ideas in a simpler, more understandable way. In addition we put some of these concepts into different terms. The basic idea is to express it, more or less the way you'd say it face to face with someone else.

If you have trouble doing this, go off by yourself, imagine somebody is sitting across from you, and say it out loud, then go back and write it that way.

Let's try one more: *Those with the measurable traits of potential salesmen should be recognized and given opportunity where feasible to encounter the buying world.*

All right, in conversation you probably wouldn't say, "the measurable traits of potential salesmen." You'd probably say, "with the potential to be a salesman." And you probably wouldn't say, "where feasible to encounter the buying world."

You should simply say: *Anyone with the potential to be a salesman should be recognized and given a chance to sell.* This sentence holds your reader and makes him easily understand because the flavor is familiar. This familiar, conversational tone always has impact. Now try a bit of this.

Try making the sentences on the left as conversational as possible. When finished check them with ours.

Stiff Writing	Conversational Writing
Escape as we use it here means a shift of pace and attitude from the nearly all-embracing domain of work.	Escape means not taking work so seriously, and also slowing down, and not working quite as hard.
Some people find in "dime" novels, cockfighting, trotting races, in barbershop song, a variant from the working role.	Some people escape from the boredom of their work with the "dime" novel, cockfighting, trotting races, and barbershop singing.
Likewise much time in the office itself is spent in sociability, making good will tours, talking to salesmen, joshing secretaries.	In the office you frequently chat with the people nearby, visit with others around the office, flirt with the secretaries, or talk to the salesmen who come in.
The seasonal and geographic limitations that in the earlier period narrowed food variations for all but the very rich have now been largely done away with by the network of distribution and the techniques of food preservation.	Because we can now keep food longer and get it there faster people can have almost any kind of fresh food they want no matter what time of year it is or where they live.
There are many managers who do not content themselves with allowing top management and the personnel department to tell workers that they have a stake in the output and that their work is important.	Although a lot of companies try, as official policy, to get across the idea that work is important and really means something to the worker, many managers feel this isn't enough and believe they too should personally try to put this idea across to the people who work for them.

KEEP THE ESSENTIALS AND MAKE IT SIMPLE IN BETWEEN

Even though some writing is complicated and technical, it needn't be hard to understand. It simply requires the application of the plain talk principles.

Instead of using a simple explanation, however, most of us work hard to make our sentences indirect and complicated. We must stop this. The rule is: Say it in a conversational way between the needed technical terms. Let's take an example:

If there is more than one catch basin being used per operation, the catch basins should be monitored relative to the amount of foreign material in them, and a large screen should be placed over each opening in relationship to the size of the materials within each basin. If materials continue to contaminate the downflow afterwards, it is due to deterioration of screening quality.

This isn't very readable, and it doesn't use plain talk. Yet, certainly not because it couldn't.

The problem is that the writer got carried away and failed to say the things in between, the needed technical items, clearly. This is pretty easy to clear up, however. Simply decide what you need to tell your reader and say the rest of it as though you were talking to him in conversation.

If you have more than one catch basin and foreign material keeps getting in, then you should place a screen over each opening. The screen, of course, should keep out any of the material that might fall in the basin. If material still falls in the basin after you've installed the screens, then you'd better look closely to make sure the screens themselves are in good shape.

The words *monitored, relative, relationship* are absolutely unnecessary and are just thrown in by the writer because he thinks he needs this tone. He doesn't, and simply makes his writing hard to understand.

George Randolph, a Cincinnati factory worker recently promoted to supervisor, decided that since he was now part of the management team he should also upgrade all his reports and memos. As a result, instead of simply saying exactly what he meant, George made even the simplest instructions difficult, making them as fancy and complicated as possible. The first week on the job he issued written job instructions to one of the crews and went on to another piece of work. Checking a week later he discovered, much to his horror, that the crew couldn't understand what he had said, tried to complete the work anyway, and had made several serious mistakes, costing in the neighborhood of $65,000.

Being an intelligent man, George realized immediately what had happened and decided to correct the mistake. From then on his memos and orders were as clear as he could make them. At the end of the year the company awarded George a $2000 bonus because his clear, concise memos and other written material had resulted in many thousands of dollars of savings to that company.

Now let's see if we can take some of this unnecessary technical material and uncomplicate it:

Technical	Uncomplicated
Learning is a process of gaining or changing insights, or thought patterns.	Learning is the process of gaining a new way of looking at something or of understanding it. It can also be changing the way you think about things.
If children are basically active their underlying characteristics are inborn, thus psychological reality comes from within them.	If children are active they are born with certain traits. And the way they look at things actually comes from within them.
A theory of learning not only reflects an assumption concerning the basic nature of man, it also represents a psychological system or outlook. Or to say this another way, each systematic psychological system or basic outlook has its unique approach to learning.	The theory of learning assumes basic things about man and also represents a particular way of looking at something.

GRAMMAR DOESN'T COUNT

The name of the game in word power dynamics is *communication.* In order to produce the greatest impact you must get across your ideas as rapidly and with as much understanding as possible. This means it's okay to use any natural straightforward method that gets the job done.

As a result there are some favorite rules of grammarians that you must now learn to ignore. The first of these is *never end a sentence with a preposition.* Actually, prepositions at the end of a sentence make it simpler and more familiar sounding to the reader. For this reason they should be used. There's nothing at all wrong with a sentence which says: *This is an assumption not everybody may be ready to go along with. This is the thing we came here for. It was a greater triumph than he had ever hoped for,* etc. Also, if you listen to grammarians they tell you never to use the split infinitive, yet this form works well in communication. A split infinitive, of course, is created by simply placing some kind of a modifying word between the preposition and the verb form. Like this: He is now ready (*to* quickly *gather*) all the crops from the field. Grammarians tell us it should be *to gather quickly,* but in many cases that makes the phrase awkward.

There are other rules, but it's not necessary to list them, for today there is a considerable difference between theoretical grammar and practical English. Simple, plain English communicates well, theoretical English gets in the way. So forget about parts of speech and rules of grammar and simply communicate in a natural easy way.

Now here are some general rules for anyone who wants to write in plain language and likes to be direct, simple, brief, vigorous, and lucid. They have been around a long time and are as follows:

1. Prefer the familiar word to the farfetched.
2. Prefer the concrete word to the abstract.
3. Prefer the single word to a group of words meaning the same thing.
4. Prefer the short word to the long.
5. Prefer the Saxon word to the Romance word.

I have a few arguments with this, but in general they are good principles to follow.

TAKE OUT ALL UNNECESSARY WORDS

Plain talk demands effective communication. Unfortunately, anytime you use more words than necessary to put the point across you are making that writing harder to read, and if you put in enough unnecessary words, you can, as before, completely stop your reader. The trick is to push your thoughts together—weed out all extra words—and keep only those needed to communicate clearly and effectively.

The authority on this is Rudolf Flesch, and if you would like a more detailed explanation of how to save words than is offered here consult his excellent book, *A New Guide to Better Writing,* Rudolf Flesch and A.H. Lass, Popular Library.

Here, however, are the basics:

1. *Say the same thing once only:* Amazingly enough, we often use two words in the same sentence that have the same meaning. For instance, someone writes: *I'd like for you to come and visit me this weekend.* Yet, the words *to come* and the word *visit* mean almost the same thing, so the sentence should be written: *I'd like for you to visit me this weekend.* This hasn't changed the meaning one bit, yet it's taken out two words the reader doesn't have to read through. There are many of these. You won't ever get them all. But try when possible to use just the necessary words.

2. *Cut down clauses.* Clauses are often like single words. Many people put in many more than necessary out of habit. Yet you can nearly always put your point across more effectively if you eliminate those that don't contribute to the meaning. For instance, someone writes: *Our friend, who was a big bragger, lived next door.* The clause, who was a big bragger, can certainly be cut down without changing the meaning. It should read: *Our friend, a big bragger, lived next door.*

   Here's another: *Any person who has a college education can do that job.* This is a little more complicated, but the *who has* can be eliminated easily, so take it out, combine the the rest, and write: *Any college educated person can do that job.* It's also possible to turn a subordinate clause into a prepositional phrase, making it both more readable and saving words. For instance: *When you come to the library, turn left and drive three blocks.* You can put the same meaning across by saying, *At the library turn left and drive three blocks.* Here's another: *As soon as John comes home we will leave.* You can save words by saying: *When John comes home we will leave.*

Now let's try it. Eliminate the unnecessary clauses and cut the writing to its briefest form. Put a piece of paper over the right-hand answers before you try.

With Unnecessary Clause	**Cut Down**
Our friend, *who was the high school principal,* came to our house last night.	Our friend, the high school principal, came to our house last night.

With Unnecessary Clause	Cut Down
Jim Jones, the man *who owns the local grocery store,* went on a trip to Spain.	Jim Jones, the local grocery store owner, took a trip to Spain.
My girl friend, *who has been away at college,* dropped into my apartment last night.	My girl friend, back from college, dropped into my apartment last night.
Billie, *who left early,* never did come home.	Billie left early and never did come home.
Any person *who is a friend of John's* is a friend of mine.	Any friend of John's is a friend of mine.
We'll be ready as soon as you finish that project.	We'll be ready when you finish that project.
We'll be ready to go by the time you finish that project.	We'll be ready to go when you finish that project.
In order to get the most out of this lesson you must study it thoroughly.	To get the most out of this lesson you must study it thoroughly.
He went to school so that he could become a doctor.	He went to school to become a doctor.

3. *Say It Directly:* Much writing is confusing because the thought does not go directly in a straight line from one end of a sentence to another. Anytime you take your reader on a round-about-path, you slow the writing down and make it boring and difficult. Therefore ask yourself, "Is this the most direct way to say what I've written, and is the main thought a straight line from one end of the sentence to the other?" Some sentences, of course, won't lend themselves to this treatment, but others will. To do this, often you will need to change the ending of at least one word in that sentence.

Now, if someone writes: *They gave us a welcome that warmed out hearts,* they are taking the reader on a circular path. To fix the sentence, change the ending of the word "warm," combine it with hearts, and zero right into the point like this: *They gave us a heartwarming welcome.* One more: *They welcomed the boss at the station with an enthusiasm that amazed everybody.* The first part is very direct. The second part isn't. Change the word *amazed* to *amazing* and write the sentence in a straight line: *They welcomed the boss at the station with amazing enthusiasm.* Now try it yourself.

Slow Sentence	Direct Sentence
Not everybody likes it when he has to shop in a store that is crowded.	Not everybody likes to shop in a crowded store.
I was waiting at the counter for my wife until I became impatient.	Waiting at the counter for my wife, I grew impatient.
That was a dinner I could really enjoy.	That was a really enjoyable dinner.
That was a girl who was a delight.	That was a delightful girl.
He was held prisoner in a room without windows.	He was held prisoner in a windowless room.
We woke up to a sky without any clouds.	We woke up to a cloudless sky.
That road was not crowded at all.	That road was uncrowded.
I could tell that he was far from being happy.	I could tell that he was unhappy.
He stared at me with an expression that showed astonishment.	He stared at me in astonishment.
He bought a boat that had been built by hand.	He bought a handbuilt boat.

In short then, the real *word power secret* is to write plainly and simply, keep sentence length in check, come to the point immediately, be conversational, and write in a direct, straightforward manner. Anything else causes the reader to work harder than is really necessary. And if we are going to eventually utilize all the word power principles we must first make sure we are communicating effectively with our readers.

IN CONCLUSION

This is the age of written communication. Unfortunately much of it is bad. Many problems can be eliminated, however, if you simply learn to utilize plain talk. Do this by (1) checking your writing with a readability index, making sure you stay within the "average" range, (2) keeping your sentence length in check, (3) coming to the point immediately, and (4) weeding out all unnecessary words.

1. *Use a Readability Index.* A readability guide that works well is to count the number of sentences in a sample of 100 words. Divide the number of sentences into 100—count all the words over seven letters in length—then add both figures together and divide by two. The piece of writing that rates between 12 and 16 is easily readable.

2. *Keep sentence length in check.* Sentences should average about 15 words. Mix them up, however. Have some eight word sentences, some 25 word sentences, some 15–19 word sentences, and a few in between.

3. *Come to the point immediately.* Simply decide what your reader wants to know, state that point, then fill in the details in order.

4. *Just talk to your reader.* Instead of using stilted roundabout talk in your writing, simply write as if you were talking to someone who was sitting across from you.

5. *Keep the essentials.* To make technical material easily understandable keep the important technical terms and put the rest in simple conversational English.

6. *Don't worry about grammar.* Simple, clear communication is more important than grammar. If a sentence or phrase can be understood clearly, by all means use it even if it clearly violates some rules of grammar.

   Here are the rules of clear communication:
   1. Prefer the familiar word to the farfetched.
   2. Prefer the concrete word to the abstract.
   3. Prefer the single word to a group of words meaning the same thing.
   4. Prefer the short word to the long.
   5. Prefer the Saxon word to the Romance word.

7. *Take out all unnecessary words.* Too many words make it difficult for your reader to grasp the point easily. To cure this:

   a. *Say the same thing once only.* Often we use two words in the same sentence that have a similar meaning. Take out one, and use just those words necessary to make your point.

b. *Cut down clauses.* Eliminate clauses that don't contribute to the meaning and cut the writing to its briefest form.

c. *Say it directly.* Much writing takes your reader on a circular path. This can be corrected by changing the word ending, then combine the sentence.

3

How
to Write
for Word Power Impact

The whole point of this book is to show you how to make your writing produce action. In Chapter 2 we talked about how to write in plain language, and this is extremely important, but there are other elements in clear communication that pretty well determine how well words get through and how much attention the reader pays to them. One of the most basic is word power impact.

A piece of writing can have tremendous impact on the reader, or it can have none. Here, too, if you do not select your words carefully and put them together in a way that holds attention your reader can quickly get bored and block out most of what you're saying.

For instance, George Parkison, a $7,000 a year Seattle factory worker, had some great ideas for changing production methods, and he submitted these to the boss regularly in the form of written recommendations. After a period of several months, however, he hadn't received one response. Then George happened to read a pamphlet on how to write for impact. The bad examples given so resembled his recommendations that he decided to rewrite them and try again. With his next one he was careful to organize well, and to state his ideas in clear, precise, emphatic language.

The day after submitting this new recommendation the boss called him, listened to him for 30 minutes, and immediately decided to give his ideas a try. The final results were a $1000 end-of-the-year bonus for George and a clear improvement in production methods. When asked why he hadn't made the changes before, the boss commented that he just couldn't seem to get interested in George's other recommendations and had thrown them away.

In another example, Bob Richards, a production supervisor of a large New Jersey manufacturing concern, became disgusted with his job and began writing letters of inquiry for a new one. After six months and many letters, however, he hadn't received one reply. That was when he decided that maybe something was wrong with the letters.

Two weeks later he enrolled in a course in written communication. For his next letter he made sure that the message was concise, the writing was active, and his use of words didn't obscure the overall meaning. The results: an immediate interest and an eventual $18,000 a year job with much increased responsibility. Written impact, then, can determine whether or not your material will be read in the first place and if any attention will be paid to it.

UTILIZE ACTIVE VERBS

The verbs you choose have more effect on the word power impact of your writing than almost anything else. When you talk to someone you ordinarily use good, active verbs that make the conversation come alive. But when most people put their thoughts on paper, they switch suddenly to passive verbs that make the writing seem indirect and unemotional. For instance, a man might say to his wife: *"Hey Mary, the boss found Bob taking money from the safe so he fired him."* But then the next morning he goes to work and writes this memo: *Due to the indiscretion of one of our employees it was found necessary by top management to terminate his employment.* You can see which one is more exciting. And after all, that's what it's all about. The more excited you make your reader the longer he'll keep reading and the more he'll understand. And this means switching from the passive to the active voice whenever possible.

This may sound hard, but it isn't. The real culprits are the words: *are, be, is, was, were, has been,* etc. These verbs have absolutely no meaning by themselves and make the reader feel like he just isn't involved.

To make your writing active and exciting, go through a piece of writing and put a red circle around every was, is, are, be, were, has been, etc. Then see if you can't take out that verb and make the sentence more direct.

For instance, someone writes: *The car was driven by me.* This is very passive. Take out the word *was,* turn the sentence around, and write: *I drove the car.*

Here's another example: *The report was written by the manager.* Again take out *was,* turn the sentence around, and write: *The manager wrote the report.*

In addition to achieving impact by taking out such nonentity verbs as is, was, etc., you can also increase the effect by selecting particular active verbs over others. Here's an example: *Johnny showed the salesman the door.* This is a good active sentence but you can make it more exciting by writing: *Johnny threw the salesman out.*

The amount of excitement you put in your writing depends on your purpose. If you're writing a note to the boss, you might say: *Our company truck hit a car on Highway 80,* but you would probably find it inappropriate to write: *Our company truck slammed into a car on Highway 80.*

You, of course, won't be able to take all such verbs as *is, are, be,* etc. out of your writing and you don't want to. In some cases you can't remove them without distorting the meaning. In others they are needed to make the sentence read smoothly. Even in the most active writing you'll find these verbs used extensively. A good general rule is to make your writing sound as direct as possible without making it awkward. When it starts to sound terse, stop; when it begins to sound passive and indirect start inserting active verbs.

Here are some sentences that should be left just as they are:

● His career *had been* subject to exciting ups and downs.
● Firing for economy may also *be* necessary.
● The building itself *is* more important than what we intend to do with it.
● Business *is* fighting for its life.

Now, let's see if you can change these sentences from passive to active, or from active to more exciting active. Put a piece of paper over the right-hand side and check the answers when you're finished.

Passive Sentence	Active Sentence
The box *was* picked up by Bob at the station.	Bob picked up the box at the station.
The company car *was* driven by Bill Hardtack.	Bill Hardtack drove the company car.
A generally favorable reaction by dealers and their customers *was* noted in the dealer pilot program.	Dealers and their customers reacted favorably to the dealer pilot program.
The theory of social intercourse which *has been* outlined in the training manual is bad.	The theory of social intercourse outlined in the training manual is bad.
That report *was* held up by Bill Gartman.	Bill Gartman held up that report.
The Graham Company's volume *has been* profoundly influenced by new product discoveries.	New product discoveries profoundly influenced the Graham Company's volume.
Scores of examples could *be* cited by me.	I could cite scores of examples.
Two new workers *were* added by the committee.	The committee added two new workers.
Bob walked rapidly into the business meeting.	Bob rushed into the business meeting.
The worker ran into the wall at full force.	The worker crashed full force into the wall.
The foreman pulled the throttle wide open quickly.	The foreman jerked the throttle wide open.
The secretary walked into the boss' office.	The secretary stamped into the boss' office.
The saw cut deeply into the worker's hand.	The saw ripped deeply into the worker's hand.
The employee ran for cover.	The employee dashed for cover.
Tom hit the boy in the face.	Tom smashed the boy in the face.
The truck sped up the highway.	The truck roared up the highway.

MAKE IT COME ALIVE

Today, many of us have slipped into a rut and instead of using good solid impact verbs—we smother our verbs by adding such endings as able, ance, ent, ant, ion, tion, ing, etc. These verb forms usually require additional words to make them work in a sentence and often have no life. *Conclude,* for instance too frequently becomes—*come to a conclusion, discuss* becomes *have a discussion, measure* becomes *enabling the measurement, react adversely* becomes *reactions may be adversely affected,* etc.

In addition, we also often insert inactive verb motors in our writing that really drag. We must then both unsmother our verbs and replace them with words that make the sentence move. For instance, we write: *Anything more than a small number of children in unskilled worker's families becomes excessive.* To make this sentence come alive we must turn it around and use a verb that has good solid meaning like this: *Unskilled workers often cannot support more than a small number of children.* Try it yourself and see if you can make the following sentences come alive. Either unsmother the verbs, replace "dead verb motors" with active ones, or both.

Dead Sentences	**Alive Sentences**
These modern Puritans *seem to be aiming* to level everyone down.	These modern Puritans *try* to level everyone.
We can give a *prediction of success* by looking at the scores.	We can *predict* success by looking at the scores.
The laboratory *believing* that idle aptitudes cause problems *encourage using* aptitude testing.	Since the laboratory *believes* that idle aptitudes cause problems it *encourages* aptitude testing.
Tables and chairs *will generally be found* preferable to desks or benches.	You *will find* tables and chairs preferable to desks or benches.
Presumably the boss *will have the use* of a table unoccupied by trainees.	The boss *should use* a table unoccupied by trainees.
The *vivid dramatization* of this situation by the case was the result of inturned visualization of all the emotions which cause people to act.	The cast *vividly dramatized* the situation because they *could visualize* the emotions that cause people to act.
The personnel office recommends a single appointment, *requiring* slightly more than two hours, *enabling the measurement* of personality and other traits.	The personnel office recommends a single appointment that *requires* slightly more than two hours and *measures* personality and other traits.
Having believed what you heard	If you believe what you hear about

Dead Sentences	Alive Sentences
about a certain employee your emotional *reactions may be adversely affected.*	an employee you *may react* adversely.

UTILIZE ONE THOUGHT PER SENTENCE

You can easily deaden a sentence by putting several thoughts in it. You will, of course, find many sentences with more than one thought jammed together, but the more this happens the less importance your reader attaches to each idea presented. If you want to give your sentences maximum impact, insert only one thought per sentence. This allows your reader to easily understand what you're saying and leads him to believe that particular idea has importance.

Try these two examples on the left and see if you can't make each idea here have more impact by putting them in separate sentences.

Jumbled Ideas	Separated Ideas
Insurance inspectors evaluate fire and accident risks and in some states fix premiums by simply passing through the factory or office building observing the arrangement of work, condition of machinery, worn belts, scrap or combustibles left needlessly about.	Insurance inspectors evaluate fire and accident risks.
	In some states they fix premiums by simply passing through the factory or office building.
	In these visits they observe the arrangement of work, condition of machinery, worn belts, scrap or combustibles left needlessly about.
Plates of the McAdory test which portrayed four modern dresses, four up-to-date sweaters, or four women's suits, at first satisfactory, became within a few years obviously old fashion and by arousing disparaging comments robbed the test of interest and of apparent worth.	Plates of the McAdory test containing four modern dresses, four up-to-date sweaters, and four women's suits were at first satisfactory.
	They, however, became obviously old fashion within a few years.
	This aroused disparaging comments and robbed the test of interest and apparent worth.

ARRANGE YOUR THOUGHTS IN BUILD-UP ORDER

Ideas become much more important when they are put in some kind of order. In addition, the impact increases when the order builds from least important to most important.

For instance, you write: *We found John in the office working on a project after we had driven all over town, called the neighbors, and even searched the library.* You can understand this sentence, but there isn't any part of it that has real impact. You can change this by putting the thoughts in some order of importance, like this: *After we had driven all over town, called the neighbors, and even searched the library, we found John in the office working on a project.* See how the impact is increased.

You can apply the same principle to a series of sentences, with several variations. For instance, you can repeat a word or an idea several times building to a climax. You can use long build-up sentences, then a short one which reaches a climax, or you can create impact by using the rhythm of sentences or phrases to build to a climax. These methods can be used singularly or in combination. But either way they give you some exceedingly powerful tools for creating impact in writing. These examples, which you should try first before looking at the answers, will give you an idea of how it's done.

Without Impact	**Sentences That Build To a Climax**
Work on daily tasks one at a time, listing them in the order you want to do them and picking out five important ones. This way you will accomplish the maximum amount every day.	To accomplish the maximum amount every day, pick out five important tasks you wish to do, list them in their order of importance and work on them in that order.
The price in effect at the time the order is received will be the price of the equipment on the invoice. In addition, equipment shipped will be shipped in the condition it now is in the warehouse without any additional work being done and without any promises as to the condition in	Orders for any equipment will be accepted with the understanding that the equipment will be shipped as-is, at the price in effect at the time it is shipped, and without any guarantee as to its condition.

| Without Impact | Sentences That Build To a Climax |

which it will be received by the customer. This is the only way orders will be accepted...

If you get stuck doing a job it is important to know where to go for help. Of course it is better if you know from the beginning exactly what you are supposed to do... and also to have a clear picture of how to start and other details necessary to finish the job. These things probably are the keys to doing almost any job right.

Tags should be pulled after the incoming parts orders are checked against the tagged orders in the file. These should have been set up by each division in the beginning because we have found a great many errors being made in ordering the multiplicity of parts for a given project.

Probably the key to doing any job right is understanding exactly what you are supposed to do in the first place, forming a clear picture of that job from beginning to end and knowing where to go for help if you get stuck.

Build Up Using a Repetious Word or Idea

Ordering *errors* are easy to make when ordering a great many parts for one project. To avoid these *errors* we suggest that each division ordering parts set up a file for that project and mark all parts orders with a red tag. Further *errors* will be eliminated when parts orders come in by again checking each order against the red tags.

Build Up Using a Long Sentence or Sentences, Then Short

Since ordering errors are easy to make when ordering a great many parts for one project, we suggest that each division ordering parts set up a file for that project and mark all parts orders with a red tag and project number. Finally check all incoming parts against red tags.

Sentences That Build to a Climax
Build up by using rhythm.

Ordering errors are easy to make... to avoid these set up a file for the project ... mark all parts with a red tag and number ... check parts received against the red tags.

WIND UP WITH A BANG

Just as word power impact can be increased in a sentence by building up the importance of a series of thoughts or a series of sentences, it can also be increased by putting all qualifying thoughts in a sentence at the beginning and leaving the important punch till the end. For instance, you write: *Stop in for your money before you go.* This is a good sentence, but the important part here is to stop for your money, so put it last like this: *Before you go, stop in for your money.* Let's take one more: *You will get fired if you leave the door unlocked.* To increase impact write: *If you leave the door unlocked you will get fired.*

Now, wind these sentences up with a bang:

General Sentences	Sentences with Impact
The plane left without us because we didn't read the message right setting up the departure time.	We didn't read the message right (setting up the departure time), so we missed the plane.
He told me to tear up his recommendation because I wouldn't co-operate with him.	Because I wouldn't cooperate with him, he told me to tear up his recommendation.
Jim is our president because he knows how to make friends.	Because he knows how to make friends, Jim is now our president.
This book will make you money if you will follow all the instructions carefully.	If you will follow all the instructions carefully, this book will make you money.

Writing with good written impact can sometimes have an extremely startling effect. Charles Davenport, for instance, a project supervisor for a small Midwest construction company, continually had trouble getting equipment shipments from practically every supplier. The company, however, was working on a rush construction job and needed the equipment rapidly to beat deadline. In this particular case, because the job was large and represented a substantial part of the business, it was almost a life and death matter for the company itself. Charles wrote several long, rambling letters telling the supplier why they needed those particular supplies rapidly and why it was important to ship at once. Nothing happened, however. Finally in desperation he wrote the president of one of his large suppliers this way: We owe you a great deal of money. If we don't get this shipment immediately we will miss our deadline, go broke, and won't be able to pay you. Rush at once.

The next day we had a personal call from the president of the company and within three days the merchandise itself was at the construction site. Not every piece of good written communication, of course, will get results like this, but every one written with impact will certainly help command attention. It is important then to utilize active verbs, to make your writing come alive by changing verb endings, to utilize one thought per sentence, to arrange your thoughts in built up order, and to wind up all basic ideas with a bang. All of these used properly will go a long way toward increasing word power impact in all types of writing.

4

How
to Unsludge
Your Writing

Making a piece of writing communicate effectively, of course, is the first step in learning to utilize all the elements of word power. You have learned so far how to write in plain language and how to impart a certain amount of impact. Now you will learn how to get rid of that writing element called *sludge*. What is sludge? Sludge is the tendency of almost everyone to try to make his writing sound "high level" and "extremely intelligent." Because of this, there is almost a natural tendency to use a long, pompous, or Latinized word when a simple one will do, to talk in abstractions instead of coming to the point, to utilize long roundabout explanations instead of a simple one, and to be, in effect, pseudo-intellectual.

A good "sludger," for instance, should be able to really go to work on a nice, uncomplicated thought like *if you try hard you should be able to cut costs*. Properly sludged it would come out like this: *By utilization and channelization of all resources available to you, it should tentatively be possible to arrive at some quantitative economization.* Beautiful—it certainly makes the writer sound like a whiz—but actually it does almost nothing to help him communicate effectively with his reader. In fact in most cases, writing like that simply winds up in the wastepaper basket. And well it should because frankly, it's awful.

Dan Bumgard, a Seattle office manager, was a sludger of the worst kind. His memos contained many abstractions and at least one long round about explanation per sentence. Comparing efficiency ratings with other offices, however, he decided he had what amounted to a communication breakdown. After that he worked diligently on every memo to make sure each was simple and clear. The result: Production increased 100 percent, mistakes were cut almost in half and (much to Dan's surprise) actual dollar savings for the year amounted to well over $39,000.

Unfortunately, sludged writing is used every day by people you'd think would know better—engineers, business managers, executives, doctors, lawyers, college professors, government workers, and more. And often when the problem is pointed out they protest that there's no way to express the thought they want without utilizing this kind of language.

There are, of course, words which compress a very complicated meaning in a single word, and the use of these is certainly justified. But it is never justified to say: *By the utilization and channelization of all resources available to you it should tentatively be possible to arrive at some quantitative economization,* when the meaning is simply: *If you try hard you should be able to reduce cost.*

To communicate effectively then, you must eliminate sludge unmercifully. Fortunately this is extremely easy to do.

Here then are the basic sludge-removers:

1. Ask yourself: *What Did I Mean by That?*

A major portion of all sludge consists of pompous phrases, trying to show off your knowledge, pseudo-intellectual writing, and unnecessary abstract terms. This kind of writing actually cuts communication and is extremely hard to understand. To put your point across effectively you must eliminate all of this.

To do it easily—instead of trying to deal with each of these problems technically and separately—you simply look at what you've written and say to yourself, *Just what did I mean by that?* If the answer is different from what you have written, then that's the way you should have expressed yourself in the first place.

Sometimes you can do this sentence by sentence, or paragraph by paragraph. Other times, the whole piece of writing is so sludged that you will need to look at big sections of it as an entire unit.

Let's look at each of these types separately:

a. *Sludged sentences and paragraphs:* Simply apply the *what did I mean* test sentence by sentence, etc. If what you meant seems different from what you wrote, then look for the key ideas and try to restate them in a simpler form.

For instance, someone writes: *A number of economies will result.* There is only one basic idea here and economies means roughly to cut costs, so what he should have written was: *costs will go down.*

Let's take another: *This raise has been made financially feasible by substantial reduction in company costs.* There are two thoughts here that need to be uncomplicated. *Financially feasible* means roughly *financially possible,* or just *possible. Substantial reduction* means *greatly reduced,* or just *reduced.* So the sentence should be written: *This raise was made possible because the company greatly reduced costs.*

You will get good at this with a little practice.

Now put a piece of paper over the *What it means* side and see if you can unsludge these sentences:

What It Says	What It Means
It was deemed advisable to consult with you.	We want to ask your advice.
We are going to *minimize the time factor.*	We are going to do it as quickly as possible.
We will economize as much as possible.	We're going to cut costs as much as possible.
It was *tentatively thought possible* to *alter the cost structure downward.*	We thought we could cut costs.
It is possible *to circumvent* the set of *rules drawn up by the company.*	It's possible to get around company rules.
Even though *extreme vigilance is exercised* . . .	Even though we are very careful.
We want to *protect the integrity* of the company training program.	We want to make sure the company training program means something.

What It Says	What It Means
To *obviate the necessity* of *coming to the point,* it has been *deemed advisable to terminate the attendance* of the next meeting.	To keep from reaching a conclusion we've decided to cancel the next meeting.
It was our *basic premise to acquire* an *elemental knowledge of chemical principles.*	We wanted to learn basic chemistry.
We regret to advise you that we no longer make synthetic fabric.	We no longer make synthetic fabric.

b. *Look at the overall sense of the entire piece of writing:* Some writing is so badly sludged that it just isn't possible to straighten it out sentence by sentence, or even paragraph by paragraph. When this happens you must do it another way. First, read it all the way through. Look for the important ideas, then try to state them as simply as possible.

This is a little harder than if you could unsludge each sentence separately, but you'll catch on with a little practice. Now put a piece of paper over the *What it means* side and see if you can unsludge these large blocks of writing.

What It Says	What It Means
We are attempting to come up with a standard procedure to make sure that the light bulbs in each hall will be changed before they burn out.	Here the important points seem to be (1) the light bulbs don't last as long as the manufacturer said. . . (2) they must be changed every three months, (3) they are talking to janitors.
Every hall is equipped with nine one hundred watt light bulbs that are rated for five months of operation. It has been recommended by the manufacturer however that under conditions such as ours that these light bulbs will not stand up as well as they would under normal conditions.	
Inasmuch as this is true and inasmuch as some bulbs seem to burn out in just a little over 90 days, we have decided to ask everyone involved to change the bulbs then. It will be the job of each of our janitors to do this every three months in his area of responsibility.	Now state these ideas as simply as possible: *To all janitors: Because our light bulbs are burning out faster than the manufacturer has stated, please make sure you change all of those in your area every three months.*

2. *Get Back to Basics*

It's certainly a great temptation to use big words in writing, but unfortunately, that only tends to make the meaning fuzzy. Sludge in writing that is created by obscure meaning can be removed effectively by making sure each word used is the lowest common denomination. That is: Use the simplest, most direct word possible.

Replace such words as optimum, utilization, tentative, circumstances, etc. These are not basic words: optimum becomes greatest; utilization becomes use; tentative become possible; circumstances becomes conditions, etc.

Now let's look at a few. Someone writes: *We are trying to increase the utilization of these products.* This isn't too bad, but it doesn't really communicate well, either, so he should change *utilization* to its basic meaning and write: *We are trying to increase the use of these products.* And another: *In our initial letter to you. . .* Sounds stuffy doesn't it? To make it right to the point and forceful, change it to: *In our first letter to you.*

Now let's try to get back to basics. Put a piece of paper over the basic sentence on the right side and see if you can find the simplest term for those on the left.

Obscure Word	**Basic Form**
Please use the right *procedure.*	Please do it the right *way.*
We keep receiving the books at the required *intervals.*	We keep receiving the books at the required *times.*
The committee *recommended* that we drop the coffee break.	The committee *suggested* that we drop the coffee break.
It has been made *feasible.*	It has been made *possible.*
It was a *substantial* raise.	It was a *large* raise.
We received the *maximum* reward possible.	We received the *largest* reward possible.
Try to do the job on the *initial* try.	Try to do the job on 'tne *first* try.
That's certainly an *erudite* approach.	That's certainly a *scholarly* approach.
That man always trys to *circumvent* the rules.	That man always trys to *get around* the rules.
Try to deliver the goods *prior to* the due date.	Try to deliver the goods *before* the due date.
Your *endeavors* are not appreciated.	Your *activities* are not appreciated.
We are *reviewing* your application.	We are *looking over* your application.
We intend to *terminate* the contract.	We intend to *cancel* the contract.

There are many more. To get your writing back to basics, simply ask yourself if the words you use are the simplest possible.

3. *Eliminate All Throat Clearing:*

This is a funny kind of sludge. It consists primarily of meaningless words and phrases that people throw in their writing just to fill space or because they think it sounds better. Actually, throat clearing clogs up communication and makes the meaning abstract and confusing. It consists basically of useless sentence or paragraph introduction, roundabout phrases, connecting words, and unneeded qualification. Bill Brandon, a star electronics salesman for small company, was a champion at stringing his sentences out. His superiors frequently complained that they couldn't get into his reports because he put too many useless things in the beginning and never came to the point. Bill ignored the complaints until he lost a couple of large sales for those very reasons.

Then, he decided to take himself in hand. From then on, he scanned each piece of writing carefully and removed every word that didn't contribute to his purpose. The result was that the memos were shorter, the time required to prepare them was cut in half, cooperation from both his superiors and clients increased and total sales shot up by $50,000.

Now, let's look at each throat clearing element separately. *Useless sentence introduction:* Introductory words can often be removed without changing the sentence meaning a bit. For instance, someone writes: *As a matter of fact, it is likely that once an employee has received an initial promotion, he will do better work.* The writer may think the words as a matter of fact have helped him get from one thought to another, but they haven't. They've simply made the reader read five extra words before getting to the meat of the sentence. So take those five words out and write: *It is likely that once an employee has received an initial promotion he will do better work.*

Roundabout phrases: Frequently writers will use big, fat, useless phrases which simply skim around the point. These basically are empty and can be replaced with a single word. While some people feel these phrases give their writing an educated feel, they actually sludge up a piece of writing and make it more difficult to read. Let's take a look at an example:

Inasmuch as we have not used the equipment in two years we have decided to sell it. Inasmuch as is a completely useless round-about phrase. Write instead: *Since we have not used the equipment in two years we have decided to sell it.* There are a lot of these useless phrases that can be replaced with a single word. Look at the phrase and see if it is as simple as you can make it. If not, rewrite the sentence. All unsludging you'll find when you get the hang of it is extremely easy. Once you have done a little bit of it you'll actually begin to unsludge all of your writing almost automatically. And after a while you'll find the habit so ingrained that it will actually be almost impossible to add sludge anywhere.

Stuffy connecting words: Words are always needed to tie thoughts and sentences together. These words can communicate simply or be still, formal and complex. The rule is if you use a word only in writing, but never in conversation, then it needs to be simplified. Saying it another way, any word used in everyday speech probably communicates effectively. Let's look at an example: *Tom left the company; consequently, Joe was promoted to manager.* Consequently connects the two thoughts all right, but you certainly wouldn't talk that way, so get rid of it. That sentence should read: *Tom left the company, so Joe was promoted to manager.*

Hedging: One other type of throat clearing that sludges up writing is hedging. For example, you write: *It seems that perhaps we may possibly be in a position soon to undertake that project.* Seems, may, perhaps, possibly, usually, apparently, approximately, etc. are all good words and sometimes you need to indicate that what you're saying isn't definite, but one hedge to a thought is plenty. In the preceding sentence take out all but one qualifier and write: *We may soon undertake that project.* A good rule to apply to almost all sludge is simply this: Write it the way you would say it. If what you've written isn't the way you'd talk to a friend, then you've probably got it all sludged up.

A few years ago a clear communication expert decided to try to determine the results of a clear writing class he was conducting in a small community. He asked every student to drop him a letter at the end of six months and tell him what they had achieved.

Two students reported their semester grades went from C's to A's. Several secretaries said that they received tremendous compliments because of better letters and that their salaries had gone up an average of $150 a month, several factory workers reported they had received commendations for their reports, and one supervisor claimed he had saved his company at least $16,000 through unsludged writing.

Now, put a piece of paper over the right-hand side and see how quickly and easily you can unsludge these *throat clearers:*

Unnecessary Beginning	Good Communication
Be that as it may, today there are few wholesalers who serve book retailers.	Today there are few wholesalers who serve book retailers.
In a like manner, Tom never goes on dates.	Tom never goes on dates.
It is well-known that the sun sets in the west.	The sun sets in the west.
It should be noted that you don't have to quit to get unemployment benefits.	You don't have to quit to get unemployment benefits.
In short, if you want somebody to do something you must tell him.	If you want somebody to do something you must tell him.

Roundabout Phrase	Meaningful Word
with a view	to
on the basis of	by
in the case of	if
in lieu of	instead
with reference to	about
as well as	besides
at one time	once
in the nature of	like
from the point of view of	about
in terms of	in

Roundabout Phrase	Meaningful Word
On a few occasions we have had to hire more men.	*Occasionally,* we have had to hire more men.
According to our records you missed three days last week.	We *find* that you missed three days last week.

Roundabout Phrase

It is our opinion that we should fire at least three men.

Our survey *has shown that* two fleets of trucks are better than one.

We are going to close down the plant *in view of the fact that* we haven't received any new contracts.

We have cut back production *in order* to save power.

Meaningful Word

We *feel* we should fire at least three men.

Our survey *shows* that two fleets of trucks are better than one.

We are going to close down the plant *since* we haven't received any new contracts.

We have cut back production *to* save power.

Stuffy Connecting Words

We recently opened a new Omaha plant; *likewise,* we now intend to open one in Spokane.

We grew a bumper crop this year, *thus* the company expects to double its income.

You don't have to turn in your report this week, *to be sure however,* I'll expect it the next Monday.

I know you're extremely busy at home, *neverless* I still expect you to work overtime this weekend.

The worker did well on the company test, consequently he was made foreman.

Conversational

We recently opened a new Omaha plant, *and* also intend to open a new one in Spokane.

Because we grew a bumper crop this year the company expects to double its income.

You don't have to turn in your report this week, *of course,* I'll expect it next Monday.

I know you're busy at home, but I still expect you to work overtime this weekend.

The worker did well on the company test, so he was made foreman.

Hedging

It seems that perhaps it may be possible for us to order you a new unit this month.

Generally it is understood that usually our policy is firm.

Apparently our records were wrong. It *now appears* you were in class on the 22nd.

We hope perhaps that when you are in town you will possibly take advantage of our service.

Straight Talk

We *probably* can order you a new unit this month.

Our policy is generally firm.

We have discovered that you were in class on the 22nd.

When you are in town *we hope* you will take advantage of our service.

Hedging	Straight Talk
Sometimes, generally you will *probably* enjoy Paris in the spring.	You will *probably* enjoy Paris in the spring.

Eliminating sludge will improve your writing tremendously. Without bothering with a lot of obscure rules you do it almost automatically (1) by asking yourself "What did I mean by that?" (2) by getting back to basics whenever possible, and (3) by eliminating all throat clearing.

Each of these is easy and simple. Run back through them quickly to make sure you have them clearly in mind. First, take a look at everything you write and ask yourself: Just what did I mean by that? If what you meant is what you've written then you've done a great job. If not, then take out what you've written and put in exactly what you meant to say. See how easy that is?

Next, go through again and make sure you haven't used big obscure words that slow your reader down. Each word must be simple and direct. Finally, get rid of all throat clearing. Throw out all words at the beginning of a sentence that aren't absolutely necessary, replace any phrase that skims around the point, toss out all stuffy connecting words and try not to hedge.

Each of these basic rules is so simple you'll wonder why you haven't always used them.

At this point, I'm sure that you've already begun to feel the effect of the word power principles on your everyday writing. With each chapter you will add more power and impact. And as you go along this unique system will literally change your entire life.

5

How
to Command Attention
on Paper

Why will you pick up one memo or piece of writing and read it eagerly from one end to the other, yet won't even start another piece—or if you start it you'll lay it down almost immediately?

One reason is that the first piece of writing contains subject material you're really interested in. (That we'll take up in a later chapter.)

But the most important reason is that some methods and ways of writing literally command attention and force you to read on, while others are put together in such a way that you simply do not want to bother beginning them. The problem is that we are bombarded by so much written material every day we literally build a barrier. Then unless there is some compelling reason to read on we say "ho-hum," toss it into our mental wastepaper basket, and stop reading. As a result, passages that do not command attention immediately or keep attention all the way through have little chance of being read. In addition, when a piece of writing fails to command attention all the way through, the amount of information the reader retains actually goes down. Fortunately there are several ways to break through this barrier and zip your reader right along with you. That's what we'll take up in this chapter.

HOW TO GRAB READERS WITH A HO-HUM BREAKER

What a useful word power tool a ho-hum breaker is. It literally reaches up off the printed page, grabs your reader, and pulls him right on into the written material. You do this by saying some-thing—briefly—that attracts the reader's attention. Then go from there immediately into the body of the writing. For instance, you receive a letter that starts like this: *In a previous letter to you we stressed the importance of properly conducting your account and asked your cooperation in refraining from drawing checks against insufficient funds.* The reader here probably won't get past the fourth or fifth word before he tosses this in his mental wastepaper basket. But what if you use a ho-hum crasher hook like this: *Do you know what happened to your checking account this time?* Now you've got him. Your reader is absolutely eager to read on. That's how a ho-hum crasher works. It must be kept brief and utilize a hook. Now here are four types you will find useful:

The Question Method

To capture your reader with a question ho-hum crasher, simply ask a short question that you can tie back into the material and which will catch his attention immediately.

If you're writing some material on car care, for instance, questions that would attract attention and cause the reader to read on could be: *Is extra gas mileage important to you? How would you like a driving bonus? Do you have dollars to throw away on your car? Will your car be a wreck in two years?* You can make these pertain directly to your subject or you can ask a general question. For instance, if you asked, *How would you like to save money?* this doesn't necessarily apply to car care, so you must carefully explain what you mean.

You can also vary these questions any way you want. They can be flamboyant or thoroughly conservative. This depends on your audience. Unfortunately, flamboyant leads have been badly misused in advertising and don't always have an authentic ring. Therefore it's usually best to keep these fairly relevant, conservative, and directly to the point.

The Striking Statement

The striking statement ho-hum breaker is simply a short abrupt statement that says something the reader isn't quite expecting. It can be very startling or just a little different. Here are a few: *Before you finish this page, over 22 people will have died. Most drivers today feel lucky to get 15 - 20 miles to a gallon of gas, but it's actually possible to get 70, 80, 90 miles a gallon and more. Everybody thinks kids don't like homework but that just isn't true.* See how easy it is. Just don't get too flamboyant, simply pick out something that is rather unusual, and put that first. You can also start with something striking that doesn't actually pertain to your material particularly, then immediately tie it back to what you want to talk about. We'll give you a chance to try this technique shortly.

Talk Directly to Your Reader

A good ho-hum crasher technique consists of a single simple short statement talking directly to your reader using the word "you." The word "you," as pointed out in Chapter 1, has good impact by itself. For that reason it makes a good ho-hum breaker. Therefore, if you're sending a note or a memo to someone, you can simply say: *Here's something I think you'll like. I'd like for you to look this over for me. Give me your opinion.* This approach, while not as dramatic as the first two, effectively commands your reader to read on.

Offer a Promise

This ho-hum crasher type again utilizes a short abrupt sentence, but offers the reader something he can only find by reading further: *This article will give you six secrets for a longer life. This pamphlet will show you how to wake up feeling refreshed. This memo will make you money.* Simply think of something the reader needs that the piece of writing can give him. Then promise it to him in the lead. If that's what he wants, nothing can keep him from reading.

The Gee-Whiz Approach

This technique again captures your reader by saying to him, "Gee-whiz, look how great this is." You'll find it used a lot in magazine articles. It goes something like this: *There are few students who can make straight A's even three years in a row, but George Hamilton of Del Oro High School, Loomis, California, has now done it for seven straight years.* You're saying in effect, "Gee-whiz, look at

George," and your reader will want to read on to find out how George did it. This can be used in many situations. Here's another: *Few drivers can get 100,000 miles from an automobile engine without some sort of repair, but actually it's possible to make them run four or five times that long with the proper techniques.* See how the gee-whiz is used?

Although this technique is extremely simple it will make a tremendous difference in the effect your writing has on other people.

For instance, Dan Riser, a $7000 a year taxi driver with a small mail order business on the side, found the direct mail pieces he used to sell his line of birdhouses produced little results. After learning about the ho-hum crasher technique, however, he got rid of his long rambling beginnings and inserted quick, directly-to-the-point questions such as: *How would you like to watch a family of birds build a nest right in your own backyard?* The results: a 15 percent increase in sales over the first three months and a 22 percent increase overall after he perfected the technique.

In another example, Alice Henderson, secretary for a small engineering firm, disliked the "beginnings" of her boss' letters, and was constantly after him to evaluate the results and try to improve them. After learning about the ho-hum crasher technique in a better writing seminar, she decided to take matters into her own hands. Within a few days the boss was getting tremendous compliments on his letters, replies were coming back faster than ever before, and sales actually went up almost $8000 a month. Although he was unhappy at first that Alice had changed his letters, he soon realized the benefits and raised her salary by $1500 a year.

Now, on the left are some standard approaches. Try your hand at putting these in ho-hum crasher terms using the question method, the striking statement, the direct address, the promise, and the gee-whiz approach. When you finish, uncover the right-hand side and see how close you've come to the ones used here.

Uninteresting Beginnings	Ho-Hum Crasher Beginnings
Question Type	
In our previous letter to you we stressed the importance of properly conducting your account and asked your cooperation in refraining from	Is your bank account important to you? It is to us, too.

Uninteresting Beginnings	Ho-Hum Crasher Beginnings
drawing checks against insufficient funds.	
We'd like to call your attention to the fact that regulation 6 states that there will be no dogs on the premises unless they are on leash. The reason for this is that several times dogs have created complete nuisances of themselves.	Ever been bitten by a dog? No fun, is it? No one else thinks so, either, so. . .
For best results, plant these seeds eight inches apart in two long rows, then fertilize frequently.	Want to get the best results possible? Here's how. . .

Striking Statement Type

We'd like to call your attention to the fact that your donation will help us send food overseas for needy children.	Think about it. Just one dollar from you will help fill a whole ship.
At the September 16 meeting, Dr. J.H. Hammershield will be speaking on the topic, "Flowers in Wood and Field." This will be an illustrated talk with examples from Dr. Hammershield's own experiences.	*Flowers mean excitement.* At least they can when you have to climb high peaks, risk your life in narrow canyons, and brave rushing streams to get them. Come hear all about it at. . .
It has been brought to our attention that tools taken from the tool bin are not being replaced. This is absolutely against the stated regulations. You will find that regulations say that tools must be brought back within eight hours after being borrowed unless permission is requested in writing.	*Unreturned tools cost everybody time and money!* When you're in a hurry to complete that rush job tools unreturned by the other fellow can create a lot of havoc.

Talk Directly to the Reader

It is difficult to do the job at the school carnival with the number of people that have volunteered to help. If we had a number of others who would help us we could probably get	We need your help with the school carnival.

Uninteresting Beginnings	Ho-Hum Crasher Beginnings
the entire job done and make money for the PTA projects.	
It has been brought to our attention that tools taken from the tool bin are not being replaced. This is absolutely against the stated regulations. You will find that regulations say that tools must be brought back within eight hours after being borrowed unless permission is requested in writing.	We want your help in returning your tools on time.
On September 30, Dr. P.J. Gogelsmith will talk about the history of the area, our pioneer heritage, and what it means to us today.	Come and learn about our exciting heritage. (Implied you)

Offer a Promise

Those students desiring to make A's in this course should read all the material in the book plus the material in the three titles outlined plus a term paper.	Here's how to get an A.
If you read these instructions carefully you should be able to expedite the assembly of this table and will find that the parts. . .	If you follow these instructions carefully you can put this table together in ten minutes.
You will find this book interesting and educational. It contains material that you probably haven't read anywhere else and pertains to the quality of life.	This book will change your life.

The Gee-Whiz Approach

It has been brought to our attention that the Forbe's unit has increased their production four times over what they have done during the last year. This is commendable and should be called to our attention.	You probably won't believe it, but the Forbe's unit has increased their production four times since last year.
The committee wants to bring to your attention that the policy put	Thanks to the committee's recommendations, complaints have

Uninteresting Beginnings	Ho-Hum Crasher Beginnings
into effect last year has resulted in 804 less complaints than in the same period the year before.	dropped miraculously and should continue to do so from here on.
The trip from South Dakota over the Plains was a difficult one. It took many days and the settlers encountered a tremendous number of hardships. This hardy band, however. . .	The trip across the Plains from South Dakota is so difficult that few people today would care to give it a try yet this hardy band of settlers did it in exactly eight days.

TELL YOUR READER WHAT TO EXPECT

Don't confuse this with offering your reader a promise. You can, however, command attention on paper by first telling the reader what you're going to tell him in a sentence or two, and then proceed to give him that information. The reason this works is that after such an introduction he is looking forward to what he's going to find. For instance, if you're writing a memo on how to check to make sure the building is burglar-proof on leaving, you will command much more attention if you first tell the reader *what* you're going to tell him, and then give the information to him in detail. For instance, you might say: *Before you leave, make sure you check the windows, the two back doors, the upstairs roof, the alley, the lights in back, and the safe itself. Now here are the details . . .* The reader knows what you're going to say, so if this is important to him he's now ready to listen. If he doesn't know what to expect, or if you ramble, he's likely to quit reading or to understand only part of what you're going to say.

USE READER GUIDEPOSTS TO COMMAND ATTENTION

Readers pay a great deal more attention when they can easily make sense out of what you're saying and when what you're saying has a logical form. If you say, "We're going to explain the four points of this job," — and list them: 1, 2, 3, 4 — you have given your writing a form that the readers can easily follow. However, if you lump all the information together, intertwining parts and mixing things up, the reader won't be able to see what you're doing and will have difficulty relating. There are many ways to correct this problem. You can say, for instance, "We'll take this up in easy steps . . . *First* (then after you finish that you say) *Next* (after which you list two or three points and then say) *Finally* . . .” These words, *First, Next, and Finally*, are your guidepost words. They command attention on paper because they let your reader know where he is, what structure you're using, and what's coming next. Guideposts are extremely important in keeping the reader's attention.

ASK A QUESTION—THEN ANSWER IT

The main problem with readers is that they tend to drift off. This means you must keep catching their attention again and again throughout a passage of writing. One of the ways to do this is to every now and then turn the tables on your reader and ask a question that you immediately answer.

This question tends to shake him up and bring him back to attention. For instance, it you are giving instructions on how to put a table together, you can list the steps, and he'll probably follow you through. But if you drop a question in now and then, you will help him to follow. If you are explaining how someone took a trip, after a particular piece of description, you might then say, and *now what do you think he did next?* This helps focus on that particular piece of writing and the reader will be waiting for the answer.

To do this, look over your writing and see if there are places where you can drop in a question that will help to catch the reader's attention—don't do this too often, but once in a while helps.

Now, try making the following pieces of writing more interesting by utilizing the guidepost and question technique. Don't look at the way we did it on the right until you have tried it yourself.

Guideposts

Uninteresting Way	Attention Catching Way
There are many things that can be used to make work easy. Work can be done when you get to it or you can use a system. When you find someone who is doing the job rapidly you often find he has established a priority and is doing the most important first, the next, etc. in order. And sometimes he establishes a time limit on the job.	There are many things you can do to make work easier. *First,* establish a system, *next,* set up a priority, and do the most important job first, etc., *finally* set a time limit in which to finish the job.
If you say what you mean in writing you will get greater reader impact;	You will achieve greater written impact by following these rules:

readers also pay more attention to action verbs. And some people tell us we should prefer the simpler word to the more complex.

1. Say what you mean.
2. Use action verbs.
3. Prefer the simpler word to the complex.

There are times when it is impossible to tell how many people will attend a function until that date. But it is also necessary to plan and prepare for a capacity audience. If there is an overflow it won't make any difference.

Since it is impossible to tell how many people will attend a function it is *first* necessary to plan for a capacity audience, *then* if there is an overflow it won't make any difference.

Ask a Question, Then Answer It

Uninteresting Way

There are many things that can be done to make work easy. Work can be done when you get to it or you can use a system. When you find someone who is doing the job rapidly you often find he has established a priority and is doing the most important first, the next etc. in order. And sometimes he establishes a time limit on the job.

If you say what you mean in writing you will get greater reader impact, readers also pay more attention to action verbs and some people tell us we should prefer the simpler word to the complex.

There are times when it is impossible to tell how many people will attend a function until that date. But it is also necessary to plan and prepare for a capacity audience. If there is an overflow it won't make any difference.

Attention Catching Way

There are many things you can do to make work easier. *What are they?* Well here are a few: establish a priority system, do the most important job first, and set a time limit in which to finish the job.

How do you achieve greater written impact? Here are a few possibilities: say what you mean, use action verbs, and prefer the simpler word to the complex.

What do you do when you don't know how many people will attend a function? The only thing you can do is to plan for a capacity audience, then it won't make any difference if there is an overflow.

USE NOVELTY TO CARRY READERS

Nothing can kill communication like boredom. A reader sees the same old thing time after time after time. As a result he really reads with one eye simply skimming across the top. If you want to break that boredom barrier, you're going to have to say it once in a while in a different way. The idea is to put a fresh angle on what you're saying, whenever you can. Let's look at a few. *This company aims to make you feel ten feet tall . . . You may think this campus is like any other, but sometimes just getting to class is like running an obstacle course.*

Breaking the boredom barrier consists primarily of saying things that are unexpected and using images that the reader isn't expecting. Try whenever possible to put the unexpected in your writing. You'll be surprised how you make your reader sit up and listen.

Now see if you can put a novel twist into the tired old statements on the left-hand side. Then compare them against the trick novelty we have added.

Same Old Method	Novelty Twist
Mothers and fathers simply do not get the thanks they deserve. After all, they have a hard job.	If you don't think your folks have a hard time sometimes, try asking yourself how you would like to try to raise you?
Since these classes have more than 30 students each it has been decided to open a new section.	If you've tried to make it into one of these classes and have been packed in like a sardine you'll understand why new sessions are being opened.
To all new employees: The company wants to take this opportunity to welcome you.	We're doggoned happy you're here.
We are very sorry you were inconvenienced and we'll do our utmost to make it right.	We're sorry it happened, and we're going to walk that extra mile to try to make you happy.
We would like to bring it to your attention that many workers get to their machines well after the bell has rung. This makes starting difficult for some of the other workers and. . .	Be at that machine when the bell rings or else. What we're trying to say is. . .

It doesn't really matter that the expressions themselves are more or less cliches, it's the fact that you've put them in an unexpected place that gives them impact.

MAKE IT OFF-THE-CUFF

As we've seen it's difficult to keep a reader's attention on dry uninteresting material. Therefore, you should try, when possible, to utilize words that in themselves are different enough to command attention. One thing that will do this is easy, off-the-cuff writing. This lets the reader slide easily from one thought to another, yet have an attention-getting quality all *its own.*

Here are a few. *It's a snap* to get the job done utilizing the new system. You can do the job easily. *Matter of fact,* we'll even help you. And one more: This system makes learning *simple as ABC.* As you can see this is a somewhat slang, off-the-cuff approach. But it's so informal it really works. Whenever you're having trouble making a piece of writing come alive—then try inserting a few off-the-cuff items in it.

Now let's try it. See if you can add some off-the-cuff words or phrases to the statements on the left that will make them command attention.

Straight Statements	Off-the-Cuff Statements
You will find that cooperating with the team will cut down the time required.	*Let's all pull together* and we'll get the job done a lot faster.
You will find that the new stencils will make the job much more professional and give it a better quality and it requires less work than before.	The new stencils improve quality. *Fact is,* they make you a professional with lots less work.
The speaker will be there to talk about Africa, teachers will talk to parents about their children's grades, and you can ask the superintendent any questions you might have.	*Monday night you can kill three birds with one stone.*
The company has gone just about as far as it can go in tolerating the situation that. . .	*We've just about had it.*
This machine is easy to handle and will save a great deal of time.	This machine practically runs itself.

USE SHORT STACCATO SENTENCES FOR EFFECT

Short writing commands attention, especially after several long passages. To leave your reader breathless, drop in a short series of items, one right after the other. Let's look at how it's done. You are writing a memo about what happened to a shipment, but about the middle of the note instead of continuing with your longer sentences you say: *We got them on Friday. We shipped them on Monday. They reached Dallas Thursday. Then they disappeared.* That's quick and effective. You can do this almost anywhere with good effect. However, in a normal piece of writing the technique should be used only sparingly. Now let's try a bit of it. Look at the writing on the left and see if you can make it command attention by putting it in short brief form.

There are times when it is important to keep in mind that we are human beings with thoughts and feelings like other human beings and that at times we can fail as well as succeed.

We are human beings. We have thoughts and feelings. We can also fail.

After having worked on many jobs for about 20 years I find I have a great deal of experience that includes typing and taking dictation. What I want to do is work about 40 hours a week and receive a salary of at least $500 a month.

I have 20 years experience.
I can type and take dictation.
I want to work 40 hours a week.
I expect at least $500 a month.

While exhibiting for one of the companies which I represent at the recent R.V.I. show in Louisville, Kentucky, I had the opportunity to discuss the contents of my first letter to you with some of the other suppliers and some of my associates that were there. It seems that the biggest problem as everybody sees it is the need for some agency for assembling the available jobs and pairing them with applicants. Probably the biggest reason many of these opportunities remain secret is due to the fact that many of the companies have no way of either advertising for these positions or handling inquiries.

I talked to suppliers and associates. The problem—no way to bring jobs and applicants together—no way for companies to advertise openings, no way to handle inquiries.

HOW IT LOOKS MAKES A DIFFERENCE

Surprisingly, the appearance of a piece of writing has a great deal to do with whether you can command attention or not. Primarily, it will attract attention if it looks easy to read. A long block of writing, therefore, makes a reader reluctant to start reading, but broken blocks of writing make it look inviting. Here now are three rules that will help you command attention by utilizing the overall appearance of your writing. (See Figures 1 and 2 at the end of the chapter for examples.)

1. Leave lots of white space at the top, bottom and sides.
2. Leave white space throughout the body of the article. This means breaking up the paragraphs. Keep all paragraphs to a maximum of four sentences. And don't use long paragraphs together. Use, for instance, a short paragraph first, a long paragraph, a short paragraph, a medium paragraph, a short paragraph, and a long paragraph, etc. Somewhere in the middle leave extra white space. This makes it seem easier to read.
3. Give especially important points their own sentence and when possible their own separate paragraph.

USE A SHORT PIECE OF DIALOG TO COMMAND ATTENTION

When a piece of writing starts to really bog down, it's possible to bring the reader back by switching briefly to dialog. This gives your writing a visual "break." For instance, you write: *Should your television require repair and the warranty has not expired, take your television with your sales ticket to any branch of the Tom Thumb Service Company for an in-warranty, no charge repair.* You can change it to dialog like this: *Should your television require repair and the warranty has not expired our service manager says: "Simply take the set along with your sales ticket to any Branch of the Tom Thumb Service Company. They will give you an in-warranty, no charge repair."*

This method works well only when the dialog is brief (not over three lines).

HOW TO MAKE IT MORE EXCITING

In an earlier chapter you saw that you could increase the impact of a verb by substituting a more exciting one for the one you originally used. You can command attention with other parts of speech in the same way. The more exciting you make the words the more impact they have. For instance, you write: *An Air Force helicopter brought Thomas Rhodes from a canyon to the road.* Okay, that's a perfectly good sentence. But you can make it command more attention yet. Try to decide what parts of that sentence you can make more exciting and just what words will do it. *Brought* can be made more exciting, and so can *canyon.* Now rewrite it like this: *An Air Force helicopter rushed Tom Rhodes from the deep impenetrable canyon to the road.* And one more: *Do you want to make good money in a limited period of time? The Time Plan may be the way for you . . . Want to make big money fast? The Time Plan is unbeatable.* As you can see by upgrading the words themselves you can change a piece of writing from ho-hum to gripping. How much you change depends on your purpose. Make it too gripping and readers sometimes feel it's too sensational and not true.

Now try it yourself on a separate sheet of paper. Then take a look at the way we've done it.

Ho-Hum	Upgraded Excitement
Poverty is not something to strive after, not a goal toward which one should work.	Avoid poverty like the plague.
The ad did not sell as well as we had hoped.	The ad was a disaster.
I search for adventure.	I stalk death.
Tom yelled at the boy.	Tom screamed at the boy.
It was good.	It was top-notch.
"Fine," the boy said.	"Great," the boy said.
The car braked to a halt.	The car screeched to a halt.
They looked for him with some intensity.	They searched desperately for him.
The boy looked upset on seeing the boss.	The boy turned absolutely white when he saw the boss.

The results of learning to command attention effectively on paper can often be extremely startling. For instance Bill Thomas, a factory foreman, was quite used to waiting weeks for a reply to his written communication. After applying the attention commanding elements for only three days, however, he was startled to discover things had really started to happen. Employees were coming to report what action they'd taken, his bosses were calling to give him answers to questions he'd asked, and communications between his department and others seemed to improve tremendously. As a result of all this, he received a bonus at the end of the first year and shortly after that a promotion to supervisor.

In another example, Shaw Benson, in charge of getting his company's subcontractors' mistakes corrected, was tremendously surprised to find an almost 50 percent improvement in sub-contractors' activities after he began utilizing the techniques of commanding attention on paper. Just this one change he estimated resulted in a $75,000 savings within the first six months.

And Vera Thomas, in charge of recruiting personnel by mail for a large concern, found a 45 percent increase in replies after application of the attention commanding technique. The quality of the personnel that the company got actually improved tremendously and Vera soon received an award for outstanding achievement and a $700 bonus.

The attention commanding elements, then, can be of tremendous practical importance and are an essential element in the overall word power technique. The Word Power Dynamics approach, of course, is unique with this book and offers for the first time an easy, non-technical way of improving your writing that really gets results. With the addition of the word power tools outlined in this chapter, you will notice immediate improvement in your everyday writing. And in each additional chapter you read, the word power techniques presented will show up almost automatically in everything you write.

Figure 1: Poor Use of Appearance

Dear Customer,

To assure you of continuing the in-warranty and after-warranty service to you for your portable television, arrangements have been made to continue the service through the local branches of Tom Thumb Service Company.

Should your television require repair and the warranty has not expired, take your television with your sales ticket to any branch of Tom Thumb Service Company for an in-warranty, no charge repair. If the warranty has expired and your television requires repair, we recommend Tom Thumb Service Company most highly as they are one of the largest, most reliable, and competent service organizations in existence today. We are sure you will be pleased with their service. See attached listing for local branches.

Service or repairs made by companies other than Tom Thumb Service Company, within the warranty period, is not recommended, recognized, or authorized by Big Stores, and the responsibility for such repairs and cost thereof is that of the television set owner.

We thank you for your past patronage and wish to assure you that should you require assistance you will find us ready to be of assistance to you. Please do not hesitate to contact us at the above address.

Very truly yours,

John DeAngelis
Customer Service Department Mgr.

EH/ps

Figure 2: Better Use Of Appearance

Dear Customer,

We want to assure you that your television warranty and after-warranty television service will be continued.

We have made arrangements to continue this service through the local branches of the Tom Thumb Service Company. Should your television require repair and the warranty has not expired, take your television with your sales ticket to any branch of Tom Thumb Service Company for an in-warranty, no charge repair.

If your warranty has expired. . .

We recommend Tom Thumb Service Company most highly as they are one of the largest, most reliable and competent service organizations in existence today. We are sure you will be pleased.

See attached listing for local branches.

Service or repairs made by companies other than Tom Thumb Service Company, within the warranty period, is not recommended, recognized, or authorized by Big Stores and the responsibility for such repairs and cost thereof is that of the television set owner.

We thank you for your past patronage and wish to assure you that should you require assistance you will find us ready to be of assistance to you.

Please do not hesitate to contact us at the above address.

Very truly yours,

John DeAngelis
Customer Service Department Mgr.

EH/ps

6

Developing
the Word Power
of Goal Direction

If you are now utilizing the word power principles we've taken up this far, you have already noticed a tremendous difference in your everyday writing. There is no doubt that the word power principles, when applied, can literally produce miraculous results.

In this chapter we're going to take up another extremely important word power principle: goal direction.

To make your writing produce results, you must take your reader with you every inch of the way. You can't possibly do this, however, if you yourself don't know where you're going. You have undoubtedly read pieces of writing in the past that you couldn't quite understand. The writer talked about a number of things, but he didn't seem to make any real point or tie the writing together in any way so it made much sense. His problem was lack of direction. The writer himself didn't have a clear purpose in mind when he sat down to write. As a result he wandered all over the place and went in several directions without accomplishing anything. The problem is that in order to put the point across effectively and get action, every piece of writing must have a purpose. And you must bring that purpose out effectively all the way through.

Wally Hamilton, the owner of a small Cleveland pipe factory, didn't understand at all the need to use goal direction. As a result his memos to employees had several purposes and were extremely confusing. Employees often ordered the wrong materials, sometimes turned out pipes to the wrong specifications, and even shipped to the wrong customer.

Wally didn't understand what was happening until one evening he sat down and reread a number of his own memos. Seeing them from this point of view, he suddenly realized that they were extremely ambiguous and could easily be misconstrued. From then on he took great pains to give each individual piece of writing an overall goal and to make sure that everything he said in that particular piece of writing pointed toward that goal.

At first Wally found it extremely difficult but with a little effort the memos began to get better. Gradually employee mistakes began to drop off, and by the end of the first year he had achieved an estimated $43,000 savings from the application of that one word power principle alone.

MAKE EVERY PIECE OF WRITING HAVE A PURPOSE

No matter what you do to get effective results, every piece of writing must have a purpose. That purpose can be simply to say hello to the folks, to get a job, to give instructions to a subordinate, or whatever. But no matter what you're doing, the reason why you're writing must be readily apparent. For instance, you write:

> *Applicants should be paired up with available jobs. It seems a shame something can't be done about it. I'm afraid you and I can't figure it out. These opportunities now remain secret. Sometimes people go through life with a lot of talents. I talked to a number of companies at a convention I recently attended. A volunteer agency sounds like a good idea.*

What an awful hodgepodge that is. This piece of writing has a very vague purpose and as a result you're not at all sure what point the writer is trying to make or if he wants you to do anything. To make it vital and important you must give it a well defined purpose, like this:

> *I want you to do something now. Because until you or I or someone can figure out a way to pair up applicants I'm*

afraid many of these opportunities will remain secret. Will you try setting up a volunteer agency?

Now your reader can see what your purpose is.

Of course, the purpose doesn't have to be to get him to do something. It can be almost anything. In addition, you may build this purpose over two, three, four, or five paragraphs, or even several pages, but you must make sure you have a purpose and that purpose must be made crystal clear.

See if you can give these sentences on the left some purpose. When you're through compare them with the purpose we have given them on the right.

No Purpose	Purpose
There are times when we don't understand each other and when it doesn't seem possible that we'll ever understand each other because we are so far apart.	I want to try to understand you but there are times when it seems we're so far apart that it's impossible. However, why don't we try again?
Things haven't been the same since you left and may not ever be the same.	I want you to come back. Things haven't been the same since you left and may not be the same if you stay away.
This card is for your R 306 toaster. There is a 30 day limit.	Your warranty will not be valid unless you send in the B 4065 card within 30 days after you purchase your toaster. Be sure to do it within this time limit.
People sometimes buy the R-10 product. It seems pretty good in the garden. Most bugs die within a few days.	If you're troubled by bugs the R-10 will help you get rid of them within a few days.
It was a good day for a picnic. It wasn't too warm or too cold. The Folsom Lake water was nice too. And the sky was blue.	We had a picnic at Folsom Lake.
The Broadman motors are equipped with air cleaners that sit on top. Sometimes it is possible for these to go a long time without changing. The motors themselves are painted black	Change the air cleaners on the Broadman motors every 60 days.

No Purpose

and often get dirty. This dirt can get
into the aircleaners making a
problem. Inasmuch as this happens
the cleaners should be changed.
Every 60 days is probably a good
time interval.

These examples are brief because of lack of space. Many times,
however, you will need more room to put your point across. That
doesn't matter. But you must make sure there is an overall purpose.

And if what you've written contains sentences that don't
contribute to this overall purpose then you must take them out.
They absolutely don't belong there.

HOW TO DECIDE ON A PURPOSE

The problem is that most people simply sit down and start to
write. They are extremely vague on what they intend to accomplish.
This causes fuzziness, makes your reader undecided about what
you're trying to say, keeps your material from coming through
clearly, and, in general, doesn't inspire him to take any action at all.
The way to solve these problems is to decide in the first place exactly
what you're trying to do.

For instance, Harvey Gallendar, a Detroit department store
employee, moved into a new home in a two year old subdivision, put
his children in school, and settled down to enjoy life. Just about that
time, (even though another builder had started to put up several
hundred new homes in that area) the school board decided to close
the school to all students but those in the third, fourth, and fifth
grades and send the others elsewhere. This meant that Harvey's
children would have to spend an extra hour and a half a day getting
to school and that they would have to go to school under extremely
crowded conditions. In addition, because of the new homes there
would be many more children using the already overcrowded
facilities.

A group of neighbors met at Harvey's house to protest. In
addition to attending a school board meeting they asked Harvey to
write a letter of protest that could be read before the board. When
Harvey sat down to write the letter he rambled on about too many

children in the schools, the fact that the neighbors were mad at the school board, that he had come here to escape from crowded conditions, that there were too many new homes in the area, that there were too many children in the neighborhood, and a number of other things. Fortunately, before sending it off he asked another neighbor to read it just to see how it would sound. The neighbor pointed out to Harvey that he couldn't figure out exactly what the letter was all about and it didn't particularly ask for anything.

That started Harvey to thinking. After all, if he expected some action from that letter it should have a purpose and that purpose should be extremely clear to his readers (in this case the school board). Harvey then sat down and decided exactly what the most important objectives were. He listed those and asked for action.

His letter, in effect, told the board he felt the school should stay open because it was already overcrowded, there would be many more students coming into the neighborhood, and it was too much to ask the younger grades to commute for long periods of time.

When the letter was actually read at the board meeting it was so definite and clear and presented the arguments so well that the board immediately rescinded their previous decision with very little additional discussion.

In this school board example, of course, you could have had several purposes. You could (1) attack the new homes going in and try to stop their construction. (2) You could lambast the school board for their decision and try to get it reversed. (3) You could ask the school board for another school. (4) You could work out a plan to bus the children in the new homes to school outside the area, or you could decide that you wanted to do a number of other things.

To be effective you can only concentrate on one main purpose, and you must make up your mind. The problem a lot of people have is that they try to cover a number of purposes in one written communication. This simply blunts the impact. (See Figure 1, p. 91). Think over (or write down) the various possibilities, and then decide on the one you really want to emphasize. That's what you'll take up in your written communication. Anything else in that particular piece of writing will have very minor emphasis. Figure 2 on p. 92 shows you one way this could be written.

Goals can be narrow, such as the aforementioned, or broad. In the school example, for instance, instead of trying to get a new

school, you might protest about the overall problem of not coor-
dinating schools and the growth of the community, in which case
you can cover each and every point listed. It's not important what
the goal is, but that you pick a goal which will cover your entire
purpose and then stick to that. This makes it more unified because
even though you cover a number of points you tie them all back to a
single theme. This gives it a lot more impact.

HOW TO ORGANIZE FOR GOAL ACHIEVEMENT

Once you've decided on a purpose, you must then organize the
entire piece of writing so it will achieve that purpose. Fortunately
there is an easy way to do it. First, decide on your goal purpose.
After that jot down quickly the main points that you intend to put
in that particular piece of writing. You can do this mentally as well
as on paper, but if you do it on paper first a few times it will then
become almost a habit.

Then look at each item with the purpose in mind. If you have
an item that you intended to discuss that simply doesn't fit into the
goal, remove it. It doesn't belong there and will take away from the
overall impact.

For instance, you want to write a letter to the principal to tell
him that you feel they shouldn't keep the kids after school. That is
your purpose. The things that come to your mind when you think
about this communication are:

1) It keeps the children from doing the chores around the
   house.

2) They get home late and are grouchy.

3) They miss the bus and you have to come after them.

4) They get overtired.

5) You feel the school is just being cranky.

6) You simply get irritated.

7) Tommy Jones, the boy down the street, doesn't get kept
   after school and it isn't fair.

Now, go back through with your purpose in mind to tell the
principal the legitimate reasons why they shouldn't keep the kids

after school and cross out the rest. This will probably leave you with such things as:

1) The children miss the bus and you have to go quite a ways out of your way after them.

2) The kids get overtired.

As you can see then, you're justified only in putting in those things which contribute legitimately to the purpose but you aren't entitled to bring in the kitchen sink or items that are completely irrelevant.

MAKE EACH PARAGRAPH LEAD IN A GOAL DIRECTION

Any paragraph which doesn't contribute directly to your goal dilutes the effect of what you've written and takes away from the impact. Therefore, it should not be there.

Now let's take an example. Say your goal is to ask the foreman's help in getting tools put away in the shop. In communicating about this you want to:

1) Point out that tools have been left lying around.

2) Point out problems involved when the tools are left lying around.

3) Ask for cooperation in helping to put them away.

Now write the letter and see what happens:

Recently I noticed there were a number of tools lying around on the shop floor.

At lunch time I also saw a lot of workers sitting around and wondered what these workers were doing. It looks pretty sloppy to see everybody eating lunch in that room.

By leaving tools around they are not there when the next session comes in nor are they there when they are needed to do a job.

I would certainly like to have your help in asking the workers to put them away when they're through.

The first paragraph is OK. It contributes to the purpose. The second, however, has nothing at all to do with putting the tools away or in asking them to put away. Therefore, for impact it must be removed. Paragraphs that do not contribute to the overall goals just do not belong there.

There is, however, a trick that you can use to overcome this. The rule is also that a paragraph which does not contribute directly to the goal can be made effective if you see it through the eyes of the goal itself. Now let's try the example above and see what happens.

> *Recently we noticed that there were a number of tools lying around on the shop floor. By leaving tools around in this manner they are not available when the next session comes in nor are they there when you want to do the job.*
>
> *At lunchtime I saw a lot of workers sitting around eating lunch and wondered if perhaps they simply dropped the tools where they were when the bell rang and forgot to pick them up again after lunch.*
>
> *This is something to consider. I need your help in getting them put away and would appreciate it if you would ask the men to put them back as soon as they are through, even if they have to delay lunch a few minutes.*

As you can see, seeing it in terms of goal orientation makes it acceptable to use and allows that paragraph to become effective.

With the addition of this new tool you will now really begin to feel the effects in your everyday writing and in addition you will find many of these tools extremely helpful in showing you how to deal effectively with people in almost every aspect of your day to day life.

THREE STEPS TO WRITTEN GOAL ACHIEVEMENT

Step 1: Decide on a goal. Do this by either writing down the possible purposes or by making a mental note of them. Then decide on the one you feel is most important.

Step 2: Write down or make a mental note of all those things you feel should go into this particular piece of communication, cross out those that don't contribute directly to the goal. Limit the number of points that you are trying to cover. For instance, if you attempt to cover more than three or four points in a single communication it's probably too many, and you should probably save some of them until the next written communication. If you have points there that are really not necessary, then cross them out.

Step 3: Apply your goal to each paragraph and make sure the paragraph really fits. If the paragraph doesn't add anything to the goal, take it out. Or try to put it in terms of the goal. If you can do that, you can then leave it in.

If your reader can see your purpose clearly, it will increase the effect of that piece of written communication many times.

Figure 1: Letter without a Clear Purpose

Gentlemen:

My family and I are active members of STOPS—Stop Today's Overpopulated Schools. We feel the Edward Kimbell School area, especially south of Meadow View Road, is a disaster area. I have lived here for several years and due to federal subsidized housing, our problem has grown the last few months. We have 100 new homes which will be finished by September. These people are required to have two children for three bedroom and three children for four bedroom homes. School board members expressed they are for the complex school idea and are spending $7400 on a structure to house only third, fourth, fifth, and sixth grade students totaling 480 pupils is outrageous. We need a K-6 school on the Edward Markam side or we are going to have to take steps to stop these houses from being constructed until there is an elementary school in this area to educate their children. We are facing double sessions— double sessions themselves are a disaster. I was always led to believe that when a populated area was in need of a school you would automatically get one. We have fought for six weeks with the school board and the members seem only to be concerned with the Freeport Ziegler area.

Figure 2: Letter with a Clear Purpose

Gentlemen:

We need help in keeping our schools from becoming overcrowded. In the Edward Kimbell School attendance area, especially south of Meadow View Road, we are going to have a hundred new homes with many more children in the area by September. Until the school board puts in a new school the old one will be tremendously overcrowded, and will be forced into double sessions. So far we can't get the school board interested in this. The members seem to think it's more important to start new schools in another area.

Will you help us to get a new school in this area?

7

Putting
Your Ideas
in Power Packed Order

The mastering of the word power principles in this chapter will teach you to put your ideas in power packed order. And as you learn to put your ideas in power packed order these ideas will literally come alive on paper.

The human mind is funny. It insists on ordering or classifying everything and putting it in some kind of logical order. In addition, the mind easily grasps things that are familiar and rejects those that aren't. This is the reason why it's easy to learn a word that's associated with something we are familiar with, but very difficult to learn one that's made up of nonsense syllables. There's simply nothing to tie to.

These principles apply in writing. We almost insist that the writing we read proceeds in some organized fashion and it have a familiar order. Give this to a reader and he'll instantly grasp what you're trying to say. Offer him a piece that's poorly organized or in an organization that he doesn't understand, and he'll not only have difficulty reading through but he won't understand very much either.

Bill Gibson, a mobile home factory foreman, thoroughly believed in written communication. As a result, he constantly bombarded his workers with written memos. The trouble was, the memo writing didn't seem to make any difference. If he sent a memo asking them to discontinue using one part and start using another, they never seemed to do it. It was only when he told each one individually that they took some action.

Thinking about this problem one day, he picked up one of his memos and asked himself objectively if he could understand it clearly and if it made him want to take action. Halfway through he realized that this memo wasn't at all organized and it wandered across three or four subjects. When he got to the end *he* really didn't understand what he was asking his workers to do. That was enough. After that he paid a great deal of attention to getting the memo organized properly in the first place, and, secondly, made sure that it built in importance.

The results amazed him. Although he hadn't expected much impact, things began to happen immediately. Changes in parts were made within two or three days, individual workers began answering memos almost immediately where an answer was needed, and worker mistakes dropped tremendously. Within a few weeks efficiency had improved significantly, and at the end of the year Bill was promoted to overall supervisor.

If we expect to have an impact on our readers and get some sort of action we must pay a great deal of attention to organization.

HOW TO ORGANIZE FOR IMPACT

Here are the rules:

1. Get It All Down First

To do an effective job of organizing, you must first gather every possible idea that you might want to include. The best way to do this is simply take a piece of paper and think about what you want to write. Jot down every possible point. Don't pay any attention to how silly the point is or how detailed. Simply get it down on paper. Later you're going to read those ideas off and make them work for you. For instance, say you're going to write instructions on how to build and put together a particular kind of table.

You then list all of those things which would pertain to the table:

> 1) Why is this particular kind of table the one that should
>   be built

2) What's the history of this particular kind of table

3) The cost of building this table

4) Where it's going to be used

5) The materials you will need

6) The time it takes to put it together

7) How to finish it

8) How to put it together

9) The tools you will need to put it together

10) The care you need to take in handling the materials

11) What to do with the table when finished

12) The order in which the materials go together

13) How to stack material on the table

14) How to take pictures of the table.

2. Cross Out All Unnecessary Ideas

The next step is to get rid of all superfluous material you've listed that doesn't particularly pertain to the subject. At this point you'll literally begin to feel the whole concept change and take on real power.

In looking at the list of things you felt were necessary to put a table together you can see that some are fairly irrelevant. *How to take pictures of the table,* for instance, doesn't belong here. *How to stack the material on the table* doesn't belong here. If you're writing an article about how to put the table together, maybe you would need *Why this particular table should be built*—since you want to tell your readers that this table is particularly good for taking on camping trips or something similar.

But if you're simply writing instructions you should take that out. The same pertains to the *History of this particular kind of table.* That might be important if it's an article telling the readers how to build some table that has historical significance, but certainly not in instructions.

Crossing those out, then we wind up with this list:

1) The cost of building this table

2) The materials you will need

3) The time it takes to put it together

4) How to finish

5) How to put it together

6) The tools you will need to put it together

7) The care you will need to take in handling the material

8) The order in which the materials go together.

3. Group and Combine Similar Ideas

Next, to make it really come alive it's important that you cover similar material only once in a particular piece of writing. You should not mention a particular type of thing in the beginning, then mention it again in the middle, then mention it again somewhere else. For instance, you should not bring in the tools in the beginning, then bring in some tools in the middle, and then bring in some tools toward the end.

Whenever you mention tools, they should all be mentioned together and covered completely at that time. This is extremely important if you expect your writing to have maximum effect. Therefore, in the organization look it over and see which things are similar. Then combine those.

For instance, *The cost of building this table* can certainly be combined with the materials you will need. *The time it takes to put it together* can certainly go into how to put it together. In addition, *The care you need to take in handling materials* and *The order in which the materials go together* all combine into *How to put it together.* It's also possible to do this with *How to finish it,* but it can also be put into a separate grouping. When you make your combinations then once again write them down like this:

1) How to put it together

2) The materials you need

3) The tools you will need

4. Put What's Left in a Logical Order

The only real rule you need to use in getting your reader to follow you through a piece of writing is simply to put it in some logical order. It doesn't matter what that order is as long as one point logically follows the other. In the previous example, for instance, obviously *How to put it together* doesn't come first. You need to know about the tools and materials, then you need to tell your reader how to put it together, so if you were putting it in logical order you would put (1) *The materials you need,* (2) *The tools you need,* (3) *How to put it together.*

In this particular case it doesn't particularly matter whether you put tools or materials first, whichever you decide.

Now let's look at a little longer example.

For instance, you are writing a short piece on the fact that our parks are not safe to be in at night (too many muggings, etc.). Now you have these points to work with: (1) *what you can do to protect yourself in the park,* (2) *what the local police departments are doing about the problem,* (3) *what's going on in the park,* (4) *what the government is doing about the problem,* (5) *why our parks are not safe anymore at night.*

Now you can see that's not a good logical order. Therefore, try to decide what goes first and what should go next. Naturally we need to know what the problem is first, so (1) would be *our parks are not safe at night.* Then you can logically put (2) *what's going on in the park,* followed by either *what the government is doing about it* or *what the local police departments are doing about it.* (It doesn't matter which one.) Finally, you tell the person *what he can do to protect himself.* This makes a good logical order and looks like this on paper:

1) our parks are not safe at night

2) what's going on in the parks

3) what the government is doing about it

4) what local police departments are doing about it

5) what you can do to protect yourself

Now you have one of the most effective writing tools you'll ever have. Once you have your own thoughts in good, clear, logical order the rest will become extremely easy. Your writing will now be crystal clear and easy to read because you've given your reader some logical sequence to follow; when properly applied to your writing, your conversation, and the way you do everyday things this very basic word power rule literally has the ability to change the events in your entire life.

HOW TO INCREASE THE IMPACT

There are two things you can do to really increase the impact of your writing. (1) You can build in some order from least important to most important, and (2) you can give your reader stairsteps that will show him exactly where he is. This helps increase the impact of what you've written.

1. Proceed from least to most.

This is almost like the rule we examined before: *Wind up with a bang.* You certainly always want to proceed from one point to another in a good logical order, but if you both put them in logical order and build to the most important point toward the end you will increase momentum and impact. When you do this you can almost feel the importance of the material building up.

For instance, if you're going to write a memo to somebody to suggest changes, list the least important change first and the most important ones last. Here's an example: You suggest changes in the tool room procedure in this manner:

1) use a written signout
2) put more lighting in the tool room
3) remove the front counter and allow men to go in and take their own tools.

You can't always do this because things must sometimes necessarily be presented in a certain order. For instance, if you need to take down a wall before removing the counter you must state it that way. But when you can use a build-up order it definitely increases impact.

Besides building up, it's also possible to build down from the most important point to the least. This is not quite as effective as the other order, but it works because it gives the reader some logical progression.

For instance, you can list things for a secretary to do like this:

Please answer all the mail the first thing in the morning. After that, file the material in the "file" basket, then work on getting the facts together for the Masters account.

The least to most important would go like this:

In your spare time gather the facts together for the Masters account, file the material in the file basket, and most important, answer all mail first thing in the morning.

As you can see, from most important to least works best here. Which you use depends on the material and the impact created by each method.

2. Stairstep

Man's mind, as we mentioned before, must order and, if possible, label everything. We can take advantage of this by utilizing the stairstep principle. That is, label exactly what you're going to do in some sort of a stairstep order. This makes it instantly clear, and allows the reader to understand immediately what you're doing. For instance, if you say: *We will divide this material into three parts,* you have instantly given him a classification tool that he recognizes and understands. If you number each 1, 2, 3, etc., it becomes easier still. Naturally you have to keep the points under each category simple but, by breaking it up like this you can take your reader through very complicated material without difficulty. There are other orders you can use.

You can, for instance, say we're going to first examine the way things work, show how you put the materials together, and answer the question why they go together in that order. Labeling like this helps the reader make order out of the material and increases the impact.

HOW TO UTILIZE AN IMPACT FORMULA

By organizing your material, building up the order, and giving your reader visual stairsteps, you have really begun to increase the impact of your writing. But you can do more.

If you expect to get action or if you expect to make it extremely clear and important to your reader, you should not only organize it well but you should also, when possible, utilize an impact formula to put that material across. Here's one that was developed some years ago and works well. It's simple and consists of five parts:

1) *Hey There*

2) *See Here*

3) *For Example*

4) *What's Up*

5) *So What*

Let's look at each separately and see how to use them.

1) Hey There—Hey There is simply another way of saying you must reach out and grab your reader with the first one to three sentences. This is explained in detail in Chapter 5—"How to Command Attention on Paper." Arch DeVandalum, who operated a small mail order business evenings and weekends, experienced considerable difficulty in getting good mail order results from his direct mail advertisements.

He decided that he would get rid of a very slow opening sentence he was using in his sales letter and use a good simple straightforward *Hey There.* The one he decided on was, "I've got something great for you."

At the end of the first month the results literally amazed him. Sales increased by $5000 and orders poured in from everywhere. Needless to say, he never wrote another selling piece again without utilizing a good effective *Hey There.*

Now check back to Chapter 5 and see if you can write a *Hey There* for the following situations. After you have finished yours, take a look at the ones we have done on the right.

The Situation	Possible Written *Hey There*
You need the cooperation of your drivers to change the oil in the vehicles regularly.	We need your help.
You own a private forest area and you put out a notice to get people entering the area to help prevent fire.	Do you want to be responsible for starting a forest fire?
You are putting out a news letter in which you have some good things to report to the club membership	Good News. . . .
You are writing a letter to customers to advise them how to handle the warranty on appliances they bought from your company.	What would you do if one of your major appliances broke down?

2) See Here—Once you've got your reader's attention you must now tell him what's so important about what you have to say—in other words, why you are now taking up his valuable time. You should include briefly all the facts that make your point: what people say, statistics, and other material that will convince him. This is important—otherwise you have no real justification for taking up your reader's time.

For instance, you're writing a memo to a crew to tell them to get some equipment out of the way. You can tell them simply to go out and get the equipment out of the way, but that's not the most effective way to do it. You must give them some reason why they should get the equipment out of the way. The *See Here* portion for this would then say: *The equipment in the road is causing a traffic tie-up, lost time on the part of the department, and a tremendous number of complaints from the public.* This gives your crew a motivating reason for doing something. Look at one more: You're writing a brief note to someone asking for an appointment to talk to a retail store about putting in waterbeds. Under the *See Here* portion you must briefly show him why waterbeds justify his attention, so you say: *Last year, waterbed sales for the first time topped 800,000, up 342 percent from the previous year. In addition, waterbeds give a better sleep, and medical authorities attribute a number of beneficial effects to them, especially for people suffering from back trouble.* See—you have quickly established the importance. Now you can go on.

As you did for the *Hey There,* look at the situation and see if you can write the *See Here* part.

The Situation	A Possible Written *See Here*
You need the cooperation of your drivers to change the oil in vehicles regularly.	All vehicles need good service to stay in top notch condition, yet because each man apparently drives several vehicles each month the oil seldom gets changed on time and no one takes any responsibility for a particular vehicle.
You own a private forest area and you put out a notice to get people entering the area to help prevent fire.	Of course you don't, yet over 5,000 fires last summer were started in this state by visitors to forest areas.
You are putting out a news letter in which you have some good things to report to the club membership.	Our pancake supper brought in over $500 dollars, and the many other activities by our hard working members produced an additional $500.

The Situation	A Possible Written *See Here*
You are writing a letter to customers to advise them how to handle the warranty on appliances they bought from your company.	Appliances are extremely vital to every family and any breakdown works a severe hardship.

3) *For Example*—Readers are funny people. You can tell them about something but often they won't really believe you. Therefore, if you want to get the most impact out of what you're saying, you must not only tell them, you must also show them.

In other words, give them an example. Let's look at the crew example again: *The equipment in the road is causing a lot of tie-ups, a lot of lost time from the department, and a tremendous number of complaints from the public.*

Now we add the example: *For instance, last week at one time there was a line of traffic almost 9 blocks long. It blocked all the side streets and kept several of the roads in and out of the area blocked up. One of our own trucks was tied up for 15 minutes trying to get to the job site, and in addition, we now have in the office over 420 letters of complaint.* This then proves what you've said.

Or with the waterbed example:

In one case, a woman who had been going to different doctors with back complaints for over 30 years found that a waterbed actually let her sleep without pain for the first time.

Examples then give your reader some proof and let him actually visualize the point. This ordinarily drives the point home effectively. These can be detailed as we have done here, or in a short memo kept to one sentence. If, however, the point you're making is only partially clear, by all means use an example.

Now try to write some examples for these situations.

The Situation	A Possible Written *Example*
You need the cooperation of your drivers to change the oil in vehicles regularly.	One, for instance, went well over 20,000 miles without attention and as a result required a major overhaul.
You own a private forest area and you put out a notice to get people entering the area to help prevent fire.	In one case, a campfire left by a young family got out of hand and burned almost 500 acres.
You are putting out a newsletter in which you have some good things to report to the club membership.	One member, Mrs. Salter, shipped out 300 pamphlets and brought in over $176 by herself.

The Situation	A Possible Written *See Here*
You are writing a letter to customers to advise them how to handle the warranty on appliances they bought from your company.	Just imagine, for instance, what would happen if your freezer broke down or you had to put off doing the family wash for several days.

4) *What's Up*—Next you've got to tell the reader what should be done, or sum up the results or meaning of what you've already said. In the crew example you would tell him what you want like this:

I would appreciate it if you would drop all other jobs, go out and remove this equipment and open up the street again for a free-flow of traffic.

In the waterbed example you would tell him the conclusion of the rest of the letter:

A line of waterbeds would undoubtedly add to your volume and fit in well with your other merchandise.

The *What's Up* part explains the significance of the other material. Try writing a *What's Up* for the situation on the left.

The Situation	A Possible Written *What's Up*
You need the cooperation of your drivers to change the oil in vehicles regularly.	This situation can be handled effectively if you assume the responsibility for the vehicle you are driving on the last day of the month and do not return it without an oil change.
You own a private forest area and you put out a notice to get visitors entering the area to help prevent fires.	You can help prevent this by not smoking while traveling, making sure you leave a dead fire, and by not throwing your cigarette on the ground at any time.
You are putting out a newsletter which you have some good things to report to the members.	With results like this we will soon be able to buy a new fire engine for the community.
You are writing a letter to customers to advise them how to handle the warranty on applicances they bought from you.	To eliminate problems of this type we have established a hot line. If anything goes wrong within the warranty period call this number immediately, day or night.

5) *So What*—Finally you need to, in effect, "ask for the sale." That is, you need to ask for the reader's cooperation in some way. Surprisingly enough, often if you don't do this, you will get little or no action.

In the case of the crew you would simply say: *Would you please take care of this today?*

With the waterbeds you might say: *Can we set up an appointment for some time next week to talk about this?*

In other kinds of communication you might say: *Could I hear from you?* or *Would you take care of it for me? Would you bring in all the records? I would appreciate it if you would get back to me as quickly as possible.* It doesn't really matter what form it takes as long as you ask your reader to do something. In the case in which you're merely presenting information, you wouldn't ask him to do anything but would simply give him a final conclusion *We can't help you. The agency strives to help the community at all times and hopes it is being of service.* While this doesn't create action, it leaves your reader in a particular state of mind.

Now try the *So What* portion for the situation on the left.

The Situation	**A Possible *So What***
You need the cooperation of your drivers to change the oil in the vehicles regularly.	Please help us take care of these vehicles.
You own a private forest area and you put out a notice to get visitors entering the area to help prevent fires.	We request your cooperation.
You are putting out a newsletter in which you have some good things to report to the members.	Keep up the good work.
You are writing a letter to customers to advise them how to handle the warranty on appliances they bought from you.	As you see, we try hard to give superior service.

The impact formula then consists of simply (1) Catching your reader's attention right away, (2) Telling him why what you have to say is important, (3) Giving him an example of why what you have to say is important, (4) Explaining what you'd like to do or what you'd like him to do, then (5) Asking for his cooperation. While very simple, this formula will create more action than almost any other method.

Now let's see if we can use it: You own a resort and you are writing a letter to a customer who was there last year, that you would like to have come back again. Using this technique, you say:

Remember last summer? Fun wasn't it?	*Hey There*
Well it's going to be just as much fun next summer. We've put in a new boat dock here at the resort and added a few cabins and they tell me the fish have grown bigger.	*See Here*
Two of our guests went out last week for three hours and brought back five fish that averaged well over 24 inches.	*For Example*
We will be open June, July, and August, but I would recommend that if you're going to come, the best time of the year would be from the 15th of July until about the 15th of August.	*What's Up*
Let me hear from you.	*So What*

This formula works best where it's necessary to give a reason why what you have to say is important. It's fine for short summaries, sales letters, brief reports, letters asking for cooperation, and many other kinds of written communications.

It isn't always necessary to make each step complete, and if the *See Here* part is complete in itself, then you won't need an example. In a memo where you want one simple action, for instance, it's sufficient just to tell the reader what you want, like this:

Note to all truck drivers:

Please make sure you change the oil in each truck every thirty days. . .

That's sufficient, but if it's necessary to give the truck drivers a reason, then use the formula.

This formula also works fine for reports provided you make the *See Here* portion fairly significant, divide it up into several parts, and insert the examples throughout this portion. In longer pieces, however, the logical organization method works just as well provided you start with the *Hey There* portion and utilize examples where they are needed.

Clinton Anderson, owner of a small hauling operation, decided to make use of the impact formula in everything he wrote just to see what would happen. He wrote sales letters to potential clients utilizing it, he used it in his memos to his workers whenever possible, and in all other letters whenever it seemed to apply. The results really surprised him. During the first month he put this method into operation potential customers called him almost immediately on receipt of his letters to make additional inquiries. This had never happened before. In addition, employees made a number of favorable comments on the new memos, and efficiency increased almost 100 percent. Receipts at the end of the first four months were up by almost $6000 a month, all of which Clinton attributed to his vastly improved communication ability.

Like it did for Clinton, the impact formula can make a tremendous difference in the effect your writing has on others. And although you are only halfway through this book, if you are now using the word power principles given to you at this point, you have undoubtedly already noticed tremendous changes in both your writing ability and in the way you are able to handle daily problems. The reason for this is that word power techniques are also good general techniques for dealing effectively with other people.

IN CONCLUSION

To get impact from your reader you must use some organization that commands attention. You can do this by either putting your writing in a good logical order, or by utilizing a word formula.

1. Logical Order

First write down or note mentally everything you feel you want to include.

Cross out all unnecessary ideas. Get rid of all material that doesn't pertain to the overall purpose.

Group and combine similar material. Many of the points you have included are actually similar to other items. Combine these.

Put what's left in logical order. Simply decide what you feel should be mentioned first, second, etc., in some logical progression.

Impact can be increased by (1) going from either least important to most important, (2) most important to least important, or providing some stairsteps or order such as numbering items first, second, third, etc., (3) telling the reader the number of items you're going to cover, then covering them.

2. Impact Formula

This formula works well when it's necessary to convince your reader of the importance of the written material. The parts are: (1) *Hey There,* (2) *See Here,* (3) *For Example,* (4) *What's Up,* and (5) *So What.*

Hey There	Catch the reader's attention with a good ho-hum crasher.
See Here	Tell the reader the importance of the material.
For Example	Use an example to make all or part of the *See Here* section clear.
What's Up	Give him the conclusion or tell the reader what you want him to hear.
So What	Ask for what you want, or leave your reader with a desired state of mind.

8

How
to Use
a Word Image Projector

What is a word image projector?

To answer this, it's necessary to understand what words themselves do. First, you read words on a printed page and get a certain meaning from them. In addition, they stand for objects, actions, basic ideas, etc., each with its own identity.

But that's not all words do. Words also produce pictures, images, and emotions which create a much more lasting effect on the reader than a simple written message.

The aim of word power is to get the maximum impact possible on the reader. For this reason you must utilize the visual effect whenever possible. This visual effect not only gives you one crack at the reader, but two because he both understands the word and sees an image at the same time. As a result this two pronged effect produces an impact that is almost impossible to achieve any other way. That's what this chapter is all about. We're going to discuss how to utilize picture words effectively, how to turn ideas into pictures, how to eliminate collapsed words, how to use symbols, and how to utilize word pictures to prove a point.

HOW TO USE PICTURE WORDS FOR IMPACT

What we must recognize immediately if we expect words to

create an impact is that not every word has the same kind of visual power. Some words give you a distant view of what you're reading, others bring that view closer up, and still others create a very dramatic close-up picture.

It's like taking a picture of seven or eight members of your family. If you stand 200 feet back and take the picture you get a very distant view. However, if you come closer, pick out two people, and shoot at about 20 feet, the details, expression, and individual image becomes clearer. Now move in, take one person, and do a shot from the waist up, and the picture begins to take on a distinct personality and the details become crystal clear. You can do the same thing with words. If I tell you there is a vehicle parked in front of the building, you get a very vague picture. A vehicle could be anything. It could be a bus, a truck, a car, or even a motorcycle, and the mental picture you have of this vehicle would be extremely hazy.

If I then say, "There is an automobile parked in front of the building," the picture gets better. It still, however, isn't too clear, for there are many kinds of cars. It could be small, large, or medium—a sports car, a stationwagon, or anything in between. The image, however, is better than it was.

Now if I say, "There is a foreign car parked in front of the building," you begin to see a particular kind of automobile, and if I bring it closer and say, "There is a red Volkswagen parked in front of the building," it suddenly becomes very brilliant and close-up, and gives us maximum visual impact. To make this kind of impact work for us, we must, whenever possible, utilize these brilliant picture words and actually make the reader throw that image on his mind screen.

What a word power tool this is! If you learn to use images properly you can literally create a picture of what you're saying in your reader's mind.

For instance, Billie Hamilton, an executive secretary for a large insurance firm, learned about the effect that images can have the hard way. After several months on the job her new boss turned her loose to write a number of her own letters based on his general instructions. Each letter communicated well, but was extremely hazy, lifeless, and often used general words like homeowners, office workers, customers, etc.

Although her boss accepted the letters he kept complaining about the fact that he felt they wouldn't do the job well. He couldn't tell her why, but he was unhappy. After about four weeks of this he began to hint about hiring a new secretary.

About this time Billie happened to hear a professional writer on a radio talk show discuss the effect of picture words and their impact on readers. Since at this point she was desperate, she decided to give it a try.

From then on, whenever she was tempted to use a general word she changed it to something which would create a picture. For instance, *customers* was changed to *teachers, lawyers,* etc. Such phrases as *We will compensate you upon loss* became such things as *We will pay you anywhere from $100 to $2000 for such mishaps as a car crashing through a wall, fire breaking out in the kitchen, etc.*

Her boss didn't say much of anything at first and then only a begrudging, "That's okay." But at the end of four more months she suddenly received a mysterious $100 a month raise. When questioned her boss simply said that her letters had gotten much better lately, and he felt that she should receive a bonus for her good work.

Now let's try a little bit of this. Look at the word on the left and see if you can come up with both a middle word and a close-up picture image word. After you've tried it yourself take a look at the kind of words we have used.

General Word	Middle View Word	Image Producing Word
weapon	firearm	double-barreled shotgun
vegetation	tree	spreading oak
animal	dog	bulldog
office furniture	desk	rolltop desk
water craft	boat	sailboat
animal	cat	Siamese
plant life	weed	dandelion
furniture	bed	water bed
tool	garden tool	wheelbarrow
electronic equipment	television	portable television set

As you can see, as we go from a general word to a middle range word to an image producing word, we go from a very vague mental picture to a brilliant one. From now on in your writing then try to produce these visual images whenever possible.

Now let's try a little of this. Take some of the general words we've already listed and see if you can make some pictures out of them when used in a general sentence. We will do this for you using both the close-up picture we've used here and another one that can be derived from the same general word. When you're finished take a look at the pictures we've produced:

Generalized Sentence	Image Producing Sentence
We were kept away from the tool room by the foreman.	Every time we tried to go in the tool room the foreman bawled us out and told us those particular tools were to be used by his men only.
	The foreman effectively kept us out of the tool room by making us fill out three forms and then taking them around to all nine section bosses for signatures before we could take out any tools.
There was a lot of light in the office.	There was a large bank of fluorescent lamps in the middle of the office and one fluorescent light mounted on each secretary's desk.
	There were two large round light fixtures just inside the office door and five rows of four-unit fluorescents which ran the length of the office itself.
He picked up some items off the desk and walked into the office.	He picked up three books and carried them into the office.
	He picked up three reams of typing paper and carried them into the office.
There were several people waiting in the outer room.	Several salesmen sat in the outer room waiting to be seen.
	Several clients waited in the outer room for somebody to take care of their problems.
Someone put some material on the desk.	The boss put three letters to be typed on the desk.
	The office manager dropped a check on the secretary's desk.

Generalized Sentence	Image Producing Sentence
He used the electronic equipment.	He dictated a letter on his tape recorder.
	He walked up and down beside the computer.

HOW TO TURN IDEAS INTO PICTURES

Objects, as we have just seen, can be far away, middle range, and close-up. The same is true of ideas. There are many words in our language that stand not for things, but for ideas. Such words as success, luck, problems, unhappy, service, and similar words represent ideas.

You have heard somebody say he has a lot of problems, or, that store gives a lot of service, or he has a lot of good luck. What do they mean by that? You understand generally, but your mental picture of that idea or concept is very hazy. And while these generalized ideas certainly have their place as language short cuts, they have almost no reader impact. This is produced only by turning these ideas into good visual pictures.

Let's take one of the general words, like service, and see what we can do with it.

When you say *a store gives a lot of service,* you see a few generalized things. But what if you say, *Whenever I go into that store they greet me at the door, they help me if I need somebody to look for an item, they make sure I don't forget basic needs, they make sure that I don't buy an item that I don't need, they carry my purchases to the car, and they even deliver if I ask them to.* Now you have a much clearer picture. Ideas, of course, require more words to turn into pictures than objects do. But sometimes it's necessary to do this when you're trying to produce impact. Therefore put yourself in your reader's shoes and ask if that piece of writing produces the impact you desire. If it doesn't then it will be necessary to turn some of the vague ideas into very specific pictures. Which ideas, of course, must be considered carefully. Now try this yourself. Look at some of the general ideas on the left and see if you can turn them into effective word pictures.

General Idea	Picture Idea
He has a real problem.	That man has a wife who is an alcoholic.
He always has good luck.	Whenever he goes to the racetrack he wins at least $300.
He is a real success.	He was promoted five times in three years and now is president of the company.
He has been unsuccessful.	He has gone broke five times in the last two years, and now the Internal Revenue has padlocked his building.
He is a real loser.	He bought a going business and ran it into bankruptcy within two months.
He is an honest man.	He found $100 on the street, then spent two weeks tracking down the owner.

General ideas, of course, have their uses but when an entire piece of writing remains general it is vague, distant, and uninteresting.

The rule here is, when you have a point you want to emphasize, turn it into a word picture.

HOW TO USE COMPARISONS EFFECTIVELY

Words that do not produce visual images are always a problem, yet there are many times when it's extremely difficult to make pictures out of words. When you feel this must be done try to find some general everyday comparison that the reader will easily understand. For instance you say: *The boy tackled the study problem listlessly.* You're going to have trouble getting your reader to thoroughly understand what you're saying. Therefore think of something in everyday life that is also listless (or its opposite) that you might compare it to. It is certainly well known that dogs don't like baths. There have been jokes about it, cartoons about it, and many people have had the experience. Therefore you could effectively utilize that comparison like this: *That boy is as enthusiastic about studying as my dog is about taking a bath.* Or you might say: *Trying to work in that office is about like trying to drive 90 miles an hour on the freeway during rush hour.* Or, instead of saying *That man's speech was dull,* you could say *That man's speech had the effect of a saw droning on and on.* Or *trying to pin that politician to a definite statement is just about as easy as trying to nail a custard pie to a wall.*

These comparisons help turn rather abstract problems into commonplace visual images. Don't worry that you're being trite or using cliches. It's a lot more important to get your meaning across clearly and create an impact on your reader.

Try these. Don't look at the way we've done it until you've completed yours.

Studying here is difficult.	Studying here is about like trying to play a game of checkers in the middle of the field during a football game.
I can't get him to tell me anything.	Getting him to say something is about like trying to get an Egyptian mummy to recite the Declaration of Independence.
I can't get up out of bed in the morning.	I find getting out of bed in the morning is about as easy for me as walking into a den of hungry lions.
I don't like to make speeches.	I like to make speeches just about as well as I'd like to have to walk across Death Valley in the summer at high noon.
I need sleep badly.	I need sleep right now about as badly as an accident victim needs an ambulance.
I don't want to see him.	I want to see him about as badly as I want to be hung by my heels over a pit of red hot coals.
Don's happy with his gift.	I see that Don enjoyed his gift about the same way a teenager enjoys his first real car.

DON'T GET TRAPPED BY COLLAPSED WORDS

What are collapsed words? Collapsed words are those words which generalize concepts in a pseudo-intellectual kind of short-hand. They are favorites of educators, engineers, business managers, and others because they allow you to sound intelligent and say absolutely nothing. Collapsed words take a specific idea and put it in rather vague "educationaleze"—some people call this "gobbledy-gook."

For instance, a sentence utilizing collapsed words might say: This building has been designed to give *maximum usability* and *flexibility* so that everyone renting an office here can reach his *maximum potential.* Collapsed words then are such words as: *immediate objectives, optimum usability, time distribution, various endeavors, evaluation of results, minimum adaptability,* etc. We have all used words like these. They, however, are not really valid concepts, but a kind of shorthand which can stand for a number of things.

Because they don't tell your reader exactly what you mean you will achieve impact only by taking these words and translating them back into good concrete terms that your reader can see. Let's look at our building example above. To translate that into a concrete picture you would say:

> *This building is designed so that walls can be moved backwards and forwards or even inserted in the middle of a larger room to give each client the exact size of office and kind of office space that will suit his needs. A law office with four or five people typing, for instance, could be arranged so that a wall separates the office space into a typing room and a customer reception room.*

Put into picture terms, then, the words become extremely effective. Use collapsed words, however, and you will produce no image or real understanding.

Look at the collapsed word sentences on the left and see if you can "ungobbledygook" them. After you've tried these look at our concrete sentences on the right.

Collapsed Word Sentences	Concrete Sentences
We want to alleviate the difficulties occasioned by the use of College adaptive advisors and...	We want to try to stop students from taking the wrong classes through the advice of our College advisors who are more interested in filling classes than they are in suiting the classes to student needs.

Collapsed Word Sentences	Concrete Sentences
The facility changes were made feasible by substantial reductions in the budget.	Because we cut out the salaries for parking lot attendants, we were then able to build three new swimming pools and a tennis court.
The building was designed for maximum adaptability so every possible group can use the rooms effectively.	The building was built with a number of accordian walls so up to ten rooms can be partitioned from the main one. In addition, there are several collapsible stages and a number of chair and table seating arrangements. All this allows the room to be made up especially to accommodate any size group and any purpose they might want to put it to.
The adoption of the resultant suggestions have allowed us to offer expanded passenger facilities.	Because we have installed an additional row of jump seats in the buses at the suggestion of a student, we are now able to carry 55 students on each bus instead of 40 students.
We are experimenting with a new message transportation media which allows us to communicate more effectively between facilities.	We are now tying notes to the neck of the fraternity St. Bernard and are sending him down the hall from room to room. This is better than trying to holler from one room to the next.

HOW TO UTILIZE SYMBOLS FOR IMPACT

The advertising industry discovered the tremendous value of symbols a long time ago. Unfortunately, they are little used in general writing. They should be because symbols allow you (in a few words) to put across an idea with a tremendous impact while at the same time imparting understanding, emotion, feeling, and a visual image. This same message, if written in the usual way, would take 50 to 100 words or more.

Symbols have the effect of providing instant recognition and instant meaning. A good example of this is the word *tiger.* And the advertising industry has driven this into the ground with *tiger in your tank, be a tiger starting right now, put a tiger in your washing machine, make like a tiger, tiger of a sale, unleash that tiger feeling.*

However, the word *tiger* brings up images of power, energy, and impact. It gets the message across to the reader immediately. And it produces a strong emotional reaction in response. There are others: break the bottleneck, push the panic button, fill a man-sized job, miracle word power, a giant of a man, man-sized, a car with some bite in it, etc., etc. It's like a jungle beat. Here is a list of symbol words with suggestions on how to use them.

big trouble	Two mistakes could cause him *big trouble*. . .
	We're going to find *big trouble* ahead.
tiger	You could tell from the way that football player played that at half time the coach had really put a *tiger* in his tank.
make it hum	The new employees *made* the place really *hum*. . .
	Like to *make things hum?* Then try. . .
happiness is	*Happiness is* getting the job done right. . .
	Happiness is just getting up in the morning.
up to the minute	We want *up to the minute* knowledge.
make history	This new group of people is going to *make history.*
swear by	We will *swear by* his integrity.
cut the mustard	That new product isn't going to *cut the mustard.*
muscle	That new product has a lot of *muscle.*
conquer new fields	Now that we're through with that project we're going to have a lot of *new fields to conquer.*

Tim Rudolph, a Dallas factory worker who made a small fortune selling a game by mail, discovered the effectiveness of symbols the hard way. Tim had been selling his game for several years by direct mail with only mediocre results. Thousands of letters sent out brought only minimal response. In making up a new sales letter, however, he asked a friend to give him some help. The friend came up with a letter using such terms as: *if you like to fly by the seat of your pants; you'll bat a thousand with this one; you'll develop a memory like an elephant.* At first reading it seemed pretty trite, but Tim decided to give it a try anyway. As a result the first mailing produced $10,000 more sales than any other type of advertising he had ever tried. From then on his direct mail sales letters (liberally sprinkled with symbols) produced more orders for his game than he ever dreamed possible.

HOW TO USE PROJECTED PICTURES
TO ACHIEVE READER UNDERSTANDING

Sometimes to get an idea across effectively to the reader you need to use more than a single image. You need to use what amounts to a moving word picture. This in effect projects a series of pictures on the reader's mind that fit into a whole concept. Since readers will not accept what you say, magazine writers use this method all the time to prove to their readers that what they're saying is true. Here's an example:

> *In a Chicago juvenile court, an eight year old girl, anxiety stamped on her solemn little face, stands mute while judge, social worker, and court-appointed lawyer debate whether to remove her permanently from her mother's care. The mother, so the social worker reports, has misused the family's welfare money and has often stayed away from home.*
>
> *The child has already spent several months in a Chicago childrens' detention center, a high-security institution walled like a prison, while court proceedings were going on. Now she may face further time behind bars while, if the court so decides, a foster home is sought. The judge turns to the little girl. "Do you want to go home to your mama?" "Yes," the child says without hesitation. To her clearly a bad mama was better than no mama at all. Our juvenile courts constantly violate the simple truth that the love of a parent or other concerned adult is as vital as food to a child's growth.*

To prove a point that the juvenile courts constantly take children from mothers when they shouldn't, this magazine writer gives an example of it happening. He in effect gives us a picture of what's going on. This isn't a static picture—it's a picture in action. You see the little girl anxiously waiting, you see the welfare worker arguing against the mother, you hear what the judge asks the little girl. This very condensed picture then brings the point home dramatically.

To really get impact in our writing then there are times when it is necessary to use this technique. When you find that you feel you need something additional to prove a point to your reader try to give him some example in action. This will give him a vivid picture rather than a dry narration. Your example does not have to be as perfect or dramatic as this one. Any series of pictures are better than none.

For instance, you say: *Tools left lying around produce inefficiency.* That's fine, and if that does the job, great. If it doesn't maybe you need to show your reader what you're talking about. Let's say it again: *Tools left lying around produce inefficiency. For instance, last week two night shift workers came in late, couldn't find their tools, and spent the next hour and a half looking all over the plant for them. As a result production that night was down.* You have now given your reader a series of pictures showing what you meant. You've shown him the workers coming in late, then you've shown him the workers looking around for the tools and not being able to find them. This gives him a very clear idea of what you meant. Because he can see it, he now believes it. Keep these examples to a minimum, but when you want to really bring a point home, pick out some good pictorial examples that will let your reader see it, state your point, and then use a word picture like we did above.

Now see if you can project a moving word picture for this generalized sentence on the left.

It is absolutely necessary to check the oil on the forklifts regularly.

Please check the oil on the forklifts regularly. Unfortunately, last month two were run without oil until the engines began to knock. This resulted in an extra $1800 in repairs.

This contest offers some excellent prizes. . . a trip to Hawaii, etc. . .

Imagine yourself lying in the sun on Waikiki beach, with the surf pounding in the background and a beautiful

Hawaiian girl lying at your side. All
this can be yours in our Hawaiian
trip sales contest. . . etc. . .

Here then you have one more word power tool that you're
going to find extremely useful in all writing. It will help you
communicate in a way practically no other word power tool can. At
this point your writing undoubtedly has already begun to improve
considerably. In addition, I'm sure that you have found the word
power tools to be extremely effective in handling many everyday
non-writing situations. As we move forward in the remaining
chapters you will find the power of your writing increasing many
times, and the results multiplying tremendously.

IN CONCLUSION

Words produce pictures which create a more lasting effect on
the reader than a simple written message. Utilizing a word image
projector effectively consists of changing words and ideas into
pictures, utilizing comparisons, turning collapsed words and generalized concepts into concrete images, using symbols to provide
instant meaning, and projecting basic ideas into moving word
pictures.

Word Pictures: Some words give you a distant view, others a
middle picture, and still others a very close-up view. These
close-up words allow the reader not only to understand the
word, but to see it as well.

Ideas into Pictures: Ideas, although more difficult, can be
turned into pictures. This is achieved by actually showing the
reader what the idea stands for. For instance, if you say, *that
man has a real problem* it can be turned into a picture by
saying: *that man has a wife who is an alcoholic.*

Comparisons: Turn difficult concepts into pictures by comparing the concept with something common you know the
reader can identify with.

Collapsed Words: Collapsed words are generalized concepts
that take a specific idea and put it in very vague terms.
Collapsed words can easily be made readable by turning them
back into concrete examples.

Symbols: Symbols impart understanding, emotion, feeling, and a visual image in one word or a few words. Symbol words are *tiger, panic button, man-sized, jungle beat,* etc.

Projected Moving Pictures: When you're trying to prove a point to a reader, it is usually necessary to show him rather than tell him. This is done by illustrating the point you're trying to make with a good example.

9

How
to Make Emotion
Work for You

Do words create emotion? You bet they do, and emotion has more power to arouse people than almost anything else. A piece of writing which radiates solid emotion produces a great deal more reaction than similar material which expresses the same thing in dry unemotional terms. You always have a hard time convincing people to do anything on the basis of logic, but put the same thing in emotional terms and they're ready to act. For instance, no amount of logical argument will make a man want to go to war, but slogans like *Remember Pearl Harbor* make him mad and ready to fight to the last man.

In this chapter we want to add to your word power tools by showing you how to put emotion in your writing and how to make it work effectively to produce action.

HOW TO PUT EMOTION IN WRITING

Practically every sentence automatically carries a certain amount of emotion. Some sentences and paragraphs, however, contain a great deal more than others. How much emotion and what kind you use depends primarily on your purpose, your audience, and the material you're handling.

Gloria Johnson, an oil company secretary, was known to be a pretty good writer and as a result got the chore of writing many of her bosses' speeches. Her first boss was quite satisfied with her work, but he left at the end of her first year, and the new man tended to be extremely dramatic in everything he did. After the second try at writing speeches for him, he informed Gloria that they were just no good, and that he would have to find somebody else to do the job.

After considering his personality and the fact that he wanted to impress every audience he appeared before, she decided that maybe what she needed here was a lot more emotion.

In the next speech she inserted words like bums, crooks, great results, etc., which aroused emotions in his audience. Added to her boss' own natural flair, the speech was extremely dramatic and when finished he received a standing ovation. After that Gloria could do no wrong and within a few months she received three additional raises that brought her salary to well over $10,000.

Just how do you create emotion on paper? It's easy. First just think of words, phrases, and sentences that produce a great reaction. Here are a few:

Terrified, he turned and ran.

With blood dripping from her wound, she screamed at the top of her lungs.

He was ashamed of what happened.

That's a pretty cheap group of people in that town.

I was hurt by what he said.

No imagination? How sad.

These of course are not phrases that you'd use everyday in an office or a work situation, but they make the point effectively.

As you can see, every one of these sentences gives an emotion that not only keeps interest up but makes your reader want to read on. In addition, sometimes that emotion has so much impact on the reader that it creates a violent reaction. How do you do this? Several ways. If you want gross emotion, look at each sentence and paragraph and ask yourself what you can insert that will create a strong response. Then simply insert that word or combination of words.

For instance, you have a sentence which says: *Tom got bad*

grades this semester. Now that in itself produces some emotion, but not a strong one. What can you add? What you can add is Tom's feelings. How did he feel about it? He could feel sad, unhappy, angry—any number of things. If you want to add strong emotion then simply say: *Tom was horrified at the bad grades he got this semester.*

Let's take another sentence: *Your performance is quite satisfactory.* What an emotionally drained sentence that is. But there are many ways to fix it. The boss can be delighted with the performance, happy with it, ecstatic over it, enthusiastic—all of these give feeling. If you want to create greater impact, then you must put in something like this: *We were delighted by the performance.* Few people are willing to do this, especially in business letters, but what a difference it makes. In using gross emotional response as a word power tool you need to keep in mind what kind of writing you're doing and who will read it. In an informal note, both business and personal, you can use a gross response. In a business or a school report you can't.

Fortunately, this is starting to change as people begin more and more to realize that gross emotion can help put the message across effectively. But you will have to judge for yourself what's appropriate. Now try it and see how you do.

The sentences on the left have very little emotion. See if you can add some. Don't look at our response on the right until you've finished your own:

Unemotional Sentences	Gross Emotion
It was brought to our attention that one of the company trucks was involved in an accident.	We were horrified to learn that one of the company trucks was in an accident.
Times are changing and people leave.	Unhappily, times are changing and people are leaving us.
Because those people tend to economize a little too much, they're difficult to deal with.	Those people are difficult to deal with because they're basically cheap.
The telegram you sent created an adverse reaction.	The telegram you sent to our office made some people pretty angry.
Your sale was noted favorably.	As to your sale. . . great!
The employees were glad to have	The employees rushed outside to

Unemotional Sentences	Gross Emotion
their old boss back.	meet him when the boss came back after a three year absence.
He turned and talked to the workers.	He turned and talked to the angry workers.

As you can see, with word power you can create gross reaction in several ways. You can do it through your reaction or that of someone else with such words as *we were delighted, we were horrified,* etc. You can do it by describing somebody or something: *it was a cheap group of people, he was a ruthless man, she was a terrible person.* You can do it by using words at the beginning of the sentence which stand for some gross emotional response. *Pulse pounding, blood dripping, shocked.* You can also describe someone else's reaction. *He looked shaken when he saw the auditor's report. He fell back in fear.* All of these work effectively in creating a gross response and you should feel free to use them whenever you need this kind of impact in your writing.

SUBTLE EMOTION

There are other kinds of emotion you can use in your writing. Every word carries some, and by utilizing those words which create the effect you want you can add impact. While gross emotion can be used in only some situations, the subtler emotions can be used anytime and in practically any type of writing. Let's look at a few words and their emotions. First of all, we can classify words as to negative, positive, or neutral. *Kiss* gives a positive response, as do *love, vacation, holiday, energetic young man, virtuous woman, candy,* etc. Then there are negative words such as: *court-martial, war, measles, criminals, rat, snake, weasel.* Some words or word combinations naturally create more of a response, positive or negative than others. Using a scale of from one to five, we will outline a basic guide here that will help you compare words emotionally.

EMOTIONAL WORD GUIDE

Positive Emotional Words

0 — little or no emotion	box, brush, place, team, doing things
1 — some emotion	vacation, lunch, eat

Positive Emotional Words

2 — medium emotion	carnival, circus, friend
3 — good emotion	gay party, happiness, joy, smile
4 — better emotion	beautiful, laughter, hug, kiss
5 — strong emotion	ecstatic, ecstacy, roaring with laughter

Negative Emotional Words

0 — little or no emotion	sleep, day, month, cow
1 — some emotion	frog, noise, smoke
2 — medium emotion	smog, cry, beat, frown
3 — good emotion	arrest, alley, spider, dark, black, frown
4 — better emotion	devil, rapist, criminal, steal, hate, snake
5 — strong emotion	terror, violence, rage, blood dripping

This Word Emotional Rating is intended as a guide only. If you want to create a positive reaction, pick out those words (or similar words) that give the degree of emotion you feel is about right. You can, as you see, increase the emotional response by picking out stronger words.

Now let's try a couple. If you say, *I have talked to many thousands of persons about their writing,* you will see that most of these words are rather neutral. But you can change this to about a 3 positive response by saying: *I have received an enthusiastic response in talking to thousands of people about their writing.* This can also be dropped to a 2 by changing it to: *I have received a good response in talking to thousands of people about their writing.* Now let's try it with a negative connotation. You can change it to a negative 1 by saying: *I have talked to many persons about their writing but with little results.* Or to a 2: *I have talked to many persons about their writing, but all results were negative.*

You not only can add emotion to a piece of writing then by selecting the word used, but you can run the scale from slightly emotional to very emotional. What you use will depend on your purpose, what you're writing, and your audience. At times you'll need strong emotion to make your reader act, at other times a very subtle emotional tone is enough.

As you can see in this chapter we are adding word power tools that are going to make your writing much stronger. From now on through the use of word power you should be able to create emotional response in your readers almost at will.

Now let's try it. Change the sentences on the left to add emotion in the following ways:

Sentence	Emotional Sentence
He talks about some of the experts. (Change to a negative 2 and 4, and a positive 2.)	Neg. 2: He always pokes fun at the experts. Neg. 4: He talks hatefully about the so called experts. Pos. 2: He talks with praise about some of the experts.
Newspapers pass along information. (Change to a positive 2 and 4, and to a negative 2.)	Pos. 2: Newspapers pass along information rapidly and well. Pos. 4: Newspapers do a tremendous job of passing along information. Neg. 2: Newspapers always pass along the wrong kind of information.
We went to a game. (Change to a positive 1 and 3, negative 2.)	Pos. 1: We had the privilege of going to a game. Pos. 3: We went to an exciting game. Neg. 2: Reluctantly, we went to a game.
A man entered the house. (Change to a positive 2, and a negative 2 and 4.)	Pos. 2: Smiling, the man entered the house. Neg. 2: A thief broke into the house. Neg. 4: Ripping the door off its hinges, the thief ransacked the house.
If anybody calls tell them I'll call back. (Change to a positive 2 and 3, a negative 2.)	Pos. 2: If anybody calls, tell them I'll call back promptly. Pos. 3: If anybody calls tell them I'll call back immediately. Neg. 2: If anybody calls tell them I'll call them back when I get around to it.

Sentence	Emotional Sentence
The boy gave the child something. (Change to positive 2, negative 2 and 4.)	Pos. 2: The boy gave the child a piece of candy.
	Neg. 2: The boy gave the child a pin.
	Neg. 4: The boy gave the child a piece of candy with a razor blade in it.

HOW TO UTILIZE AN EMOTIONAL GOAL

It's possible in a piece of writing to utilize an emotional goal just as you utilize any other kind. Simply decide what kind of emotion you want to project, and take out any word in the sentence, paragraph, or piece that detracts from this. Or, add or change to make it have the emotional tone you want. For instance, if you decide that a sentence or a paragraph must have enthusiasm first of all, write it, then look at it and see if there's anything that either detracts from your emotional goal or needs to be changed or added to.

Let's try one: *It was great at the meeting. Everyone got something out of it although we had a couple of problems at the end that were overcome.* The part about the problems here tends to temper the enthusiasm. If you want it to come off very positively enthusiastic you must take out the negatives and end on an upbeat like this: *It was great at the meeting. Everyone got a great deal out of it. It ended on a very positive note.* Or if you want to leave a feeling of doubt, simply say: *The meeting was fine. I believe everyone got quite a bit out of it. We, however, have a few reservations.*

Let's try one more. *The girl got a job at the telephone company and finally went back to work—not when she expected but almost a year later. It had taken her a lot longer to get another job than she thought.* This of course already has some emotion in it, but is it what you want? Look it over. If it isn't, what can you do to fix it? Well, if we wanted to project a favorable optimism, we'd fix it like this: *The girl finally got a job at the telephone company, maybe not as soon as she had hoped, but she was happy anyway, and the time off had given her a chance to do other things. Now she was ready to tackle the future.* As you can see we have projected this feeling all the way through. You can do the same thing with your writing. Does it project the feeling you wish? If not, decide what changes are necessary, then make them.

HOW TO USE INCREASED WORD EXCITEMENT FOR IMPACT

As we have seen before, words range from almost neutral to extremely exciting. Within the framework of what you're doing you should always try to use the most exciting form of the word possible. If you say, for instance: *The plant printing press turned out much work,* you're not getting all the excitement possible out of it. A more exciting word is: *The plant printing press, operating at top speed, poured out tremendous volumes of material.* Let's look at a few words and see how the excitement can be increased. *Produced . . . . turned out . . . poured out . . . gushed.* As you can see, this corresponds to going from positive 2, for instance, up to a positive 5—and as you can see the excitement and emotional level of the verb actually increase as you go up. Here's another: *knocked . . . beat . . . hammered.*

You won't always find this appropriate, but in many cases it is. Therefore, unless you're deliberately trying to tone the writing down, always look for the most exciting word possible that still expresses what you're trying to say. This helps carry your reader and increases the impact.

Now let's try a few and see if you can give the sentences on the left a little more impact by inserting a more exciting verb or other part of speech. Cover the way we have done it on the right-hand side.

Standard	More Exciting
He asked that the job be done now.	He demands that the job be done now.
He asked that the secretary turn the work out on time.	He insisted that the secretary turn the work out on time.
The noise level in the office was high.	The noise level in the office reached an ear-shattering crescendo.
The automotive parts came from the machine rapidly.	The automotive parts literally poured from the machine.
He likes to work with computers.	He delights in working with computers.
He ran across the street.	He charged across the street.

Standard	More Exciting
The boy threw the ball hard against the wall.	The boy smashed the ball against the wall.

HOW TO APPEAL EMOTIONALLY TO PEOPLE

As we have seen, words are not really just words after all. Some get no response. Others make people react strongly. Certain subjects or words make us laugh, cry, hate, love, get mad, or do many things. These feelings originate from past experiences or a series of past experiences. Roy Garn, a nationally recognized authority on emotional appeals technique, and author of the book *Magic Power of Emotional Appeal* (Prentice-Hall, Inc.) says that all people react generally to four kinds of emotional areas: money, romance, self-preservation and recognition. All of these move people. And the key to appealing to people is to try to include one of these four areas in your writing whenever possible.

Some people of course are more interested in one area than another. If you can recognize which area your reader is most interested in, then you can concentrate on that particular appeal.

For instance, if you say, *this report should save you at least ten dollars,* you have used an appeal to the money response. Now let's briefly look at all of the areas:

Money appeal:
This book can make you rich ... there's gold in earth-worms ...You can buy meat for one-half of what you're paying now ...

Preservation appeal:
Want instant relief? ... Need more pep? ... You can go through life with a lot more vigor ... Sometimes it's easy to take off pounds ...

Romance appeal:
To an audience of single women you say "practically every one of you will be married within a year" ... Women (or men) will really love you ... the opposite sex just can't resist. ..

Recognition appeal:
You can become a leader ... It's easy to be a better student .. Why can't you be best?

HOW TO USE EMOTIONAL APPEAL
TO MAKE PEOPLE RESPOND

This consists primarily of deciding which of the four appeals are most appropriate to your objectives and then make sure you include them in your writing. Let's try it:

In a letter you state: *Doubtless you are aware of the fact that there is a close relationship between the recent rise of juvenile delinquency and the lack of recreational facilities for adolescents.*

That sentence probably won't appeal to anybody. So first you've got to decide what appeal would be most appropriate. Money? Maybe, but it would be difficult to get a money appeal in there easily. Romance? Possible, again not easy to handle. Self-preservation? Possible. Juvenile delinquency could touch self-preservation. Let's see what we can do with that. We'll rewrite our letter like this: *Ever been held up by a teenager? I hope not because it's a terrifying experience to be held up by anybody, but do you realize there's a close relationship between the recent rise in juvenile delinquency and the lack of recreational facilities for adolescents.* Now we have added strong preservation.

Let's try another example. You write, as an officer in a bank: *Once again we have had to refuse to honor one of your checks. This time it was for $97.50 which our records show would have overdrawn your account. I'm sure you realize this sort of thing is not in keeping with sound business practices.*

Now there is certainly money here but you haven't linked it very well with the reader. See if you can't appeal directly to his feeling for money. Let's start your letter like this: *Does money mean anything to you? Well, it does to us, too, and. once again we've had to refuse to honor one of your checks. This costs both of us money.* Now you're using his money response to create a reaction. These appeals, of course, simply add one more word power tool that you can use.

Which appeal you concentrate on depends primarily on your audience and the subject you're dealing with. But basically it's simple to keep in mind that every piece of communication, to get maximum response, is going to have to include a strong appeal in one of these four areas. The trick is to decide which one fits best. Now try it. We'll give you a subject and an audience on the left. See if you can decide which of the four areas should be stressed and how the appeal should be made. After you've finished, check the ones we've done on the right.

Subject and Audience	Proper Appeal

Money

Poor writing results in many mistakes, people do not understand what's being said, time is wasted... a lot of paper is used ... *to a business audience*

Did you know that millions of dollars are wasted every year in poor writing? ... some of it right there in your office. Written instructions that can't be understood, cause mistakes and wasted time. In addition over-wordiness wastes paper, ink and a secretary's time... all of which translates into lost profit.

Tax reductions which go into effect this month have been made financially feasible by substantial reductions in expenditures...*to the general public*

We are cutting down on your taxes beginning this month. We couldn't have done this if we hadn't cut down on government expense.

Recognition

Poor writing results in many mistakes, people do not understand what's being said, time is wasted, a lot of paper is used...*to a business audience*

Written instructions that can't be understood cause mistakes and wasted time. Certainly your efficiency as an executive can be improved immeasurably by learning to communicate effectively.

The new Xo2 typewriter ribbon gives blacker copy, is easier to erase, and makes a typewritten page look better....*to secretaries*

The new Xo2 typewriter ribbon really makes you look good. Since this ribbon now is easier to erase, gives blacker copy, and makes every typewritten page look better, it's a snap to impress the boss with the quality of your work.

Preservation appeal

All secretaries will take a ten minute break at 11:00 every morning regardless of what they are doing...*to secretaries*

The company requests that you take a ten minute break every day at 11:00 o'clock. It has been found that in order to feel at their best, people must relax for a few minutes and completely get their mind off what

Subject and Audience	Proper Appeal
	they've been doing. We hope you'll try this.
All meals should include several foods with at least one leafy vegetable . . .*to housewives*	To make sure your family is at its healthiest they should be fed a balanced diet of several foods, including one leafy vegetable.
	Romance appeal
It is important to get an education if you intend to reach your full potential in later life.	Let's face it, girls like guys who are doing things . . . and those who are the real doers are usually the ones who have a good education. . .
We have some job openings available in Tunisia, Algeria, and similar areas.	Does the thought of working in an exotic foreign country appeal to you?

Now let's take a rather dull business communication and see if we can't make it come alive by applying a little emotion.

Use of large long-term investment accounts in savings and loans as profitable substitutes for AAA bonds is a relatively new but growing concept in the investment field.

The idea is rapidly winning support in important quarters as institutional and large individual investors gain more and more knowledge regarding the economic stature of leading savings and loan associations and greater familiarity with their method of operation.

In fact, competent studies in recent months comparing savings and loan accounts with AAA corporate bonds have shown savings and loans to be more advantageous from many aspects:

For example:

1. *Higher Average Yield—Over the long term savings and loan accounts have yielded a higher average annual return than AAA bonds.*

2. *No Fluctuation in Market Value—The savings and loan account is always redeemable at face value. The AAA bond, while eventually redeemable at par at maturity, may have to be sold at a time when its market price is below its face value.*

3. *Non-callable—Bonds with fairly high yield that are callable may be redeemed by the issuer at a time when interest rates are low. This can reduce sharply the investor's return when funds are reinvested in bonds. Savings and loan accounts are not callable, and while rates fluctuate, they historically provide a higher return on the average than Aaa bonds.*

4. *Greater Safety—Savings in a savings and loan association are insured by the Federal Savings and Loan Insurance Corporation. Bonds are not.*

That is incredibly dull. Let's revise it:

Do large savings and loan accounts return you as much money in the long run as bonds can?

You bet they can and although this type of investment is a fairly new one, its use has literally exploded as larger investors begin to understand the multiple benefits of savings and loans.

Studies show these advantages:

1. *Higher Yield Average—Savings and loans actually produce a higher return (over the long run) than bonds.*

2. *No fluctuation in market value—Your savings and loan account is worth exactly what your passbook says it is. It doesn't drop unless you withdraw money. But the market price of bonds bounces up and down.*

3. *Non-callable—Whoever issued the bonds may redeem them anytime he wants. If done when the interest rates are low this redemption can slash returns, but savings and loan accounts can't be cancelled by savings and loan institutions.*

4. *Greater Safety-Savings and loan accounts offer insured security. Bonds don't.*

With the addition of emotion you are now developing your word power at an accelerated rate. Proper use of emotion allows us to make effective use of the basic word power dynamic principles. And while these tools are now adding a great deal to the effectiveness of your writing you should also be aware that they will be useful in almost everything you do. As you begin to recognize the effect of emotion and the power it has to create reaction, you will be able to utilize it at will in almost every conversation to create whatever reaction you desire.

10

How
to Motivate
Through Word Power

One of the major problems in writing is to make your reader take some action. Naturally, you want to get through to him and make him understand what you've written, but that's only the first step. After he understands, you usually want him to do something: to pick up the phone, to take some action at work, to mail a letter, or any number of things.

There are, as you have seen in other chapters, a lot of barriers. The reader has a hard time wading through what you've written, he can't get interested immediately, he isn't compelled to read on, or any number of things. Now, you must learn to supply that missing ingredient and motivate this reader. Naturally you can't make him act every time, but you can make him want to in many cases. And when you do all sorts of good things can happen: you can get an interview for a job, your suggestions can be accepted, someone can mail you an order, the office will operate more efficiently, you can set up that meeting you want, you can make a school board change its mind, and a lot more.

FUTURE PROMISE

Most of us live in or for the past, the present, and the future. The past, even though many of us cling to it, really isn't very exciting. The present still doesn't initiate much excitement, but the future? You bet it does. The future is full of hope. The future is filled with dreams of great things to come, for naturally, tomorrow is going to be better. And while very few people will respond to the past or the present, most people will respond in some way to something that's promised out there in the future.

Ron Johnson, a former factory worker turned insurance salesman, uses future promise quite effectively to motivate potential clients. During the early years of his business Ron often utilized stock letters to potential clients which simply told them what he was doing, explained the benefits from the policy he was selling, and asked them to let him set up an appointment. The results were fair, but Ron felt there ought to be a way to do it better. After thinking about it a while he designed a letter containing future promise which began: *Do you want to be financially secure five years from now; seven years, ten years? All of this is possible. . .*

Within two months the responses to Ron's letters increased 100 percent, and by the end of the year his income had jumped a good $25,000.

Now, before getting down to the actual techniques of putting future promise in your writing, let's look at some of the things future promise is:

Talk of Tomorrow

To talk of future promise effectively you must whenever possible talk of tomorrow. People have mostly forgotten what happened in the past and really don't want to hear about it except as nostalgic remembrance. They basically want to know what's promised tomorrow. Everybody understands this, so you are safe in offering a grand future. Remember, however, people are not interested in talk of tomorrow as it relates to you, but only as it relates to them. This talk of tomorrow might concern the money they're going to make, their future educations, their health, or anything else. It is more effective, however, if you keep it in the four areas of money, romance, health, and recognition.

Create a Visual Image

To generate promise you really have to create an image on paper. The great value of writing is that it is extremely easy to create visual images with words. Suppose you are selling a set of tools to do-it-yourself mechanics. Now, everybody dreams of saving money by doing their own repair work, so to motivate effectively you must create an image in which it's already accomplished. You can do this on paper by merely saying: *Why pay out thousands every year for automotive tune-ups when you can do it yourself better, many dollars cheaper, and sometimes a lot faster than any mechanic?* This, as you can see, creates the image that he, the reader, is just as capable as the mechanic on the corner. While not every piece of writing can utilize a visual image, there are times when one can.

Eliminate the Negative

Future promise means saying that something is possible, not putting in roadblocks. To use future promise effectively, you must always stress the possible, never the impossible. If you say, for instance, *It's possible for you to go to Bali if you have the money,* there are a number of problems you must clear away first.

You have slowed your reader down and thrown somewhat of a problem in his way. Your future promise there is blocked. But suppose you simply say to him: *You, too, can go to Bali. Just fill in the coupon and you're almost on your way.* There are no roadblocks and it seems as simple as ABC. It may not be. But if you expect maximum action, you show the roadblocks only after the action is taken. Naturally, there are times when it's necessary to show both sides of the problem clearly and fairly. But remember negatives tend to keep people from acting. If you expect maximum action you must take out as many negatives as possible.

Future Promise Should Not Be Any Promise At All

The trick in creating action with future promise is really not to promise anything. Put another way, the promise must be something that can only be fulfilled by the reader's action. It is not something you promised, but something he can get by only doing himself. For instance, you can say: *I can promise you you'll get better grades when you straighten out your sloppy study habits.* Or you might say: *Your car will perform a lot better if you maintain it properly.* You haven't really promised him anything that doesn't depend on him entirely. This is the secret of using future promise effectively.

Now let's look at the rules. To make future promise create

action: Talk of something that's going to happen tomorrow, create a visual image when possible, eliminate most negatives, and make the fulfillment of the promise dependent on him. You can do all of these at once or any of them separately.

Let's try a few. Look at the sentence on the left and see if you can turn it into a future promise that will make your reader want to do something.

When you've tried your hand then look at the way we did it.

The Situation	Future Promise

Talk of Tomorrow

People can through study and retraining qualify themselves for better jobs.	If you prepare properly you can make a lot better money in the near future.
It is not necessary to stay in the same job.	You can get a better job. (Future implied)
People find that situations change.	The future can hold many good changes.
Some people make money from part time business.	Imagine yourself a year from now in your own money-making part-time business.

Create an Illusion

This book contains a lot of information.	This book is packed with dynamite for your future.
Some people make money from part-time business.	A part-time business can make money for you automatically.
It's possible to clear up problems without a lawyer in many cases.	Why pay out good money for a lawyer, when you can get along very nicely without one?
Some people grow vegetables in flowerbeds or home gardens to supplement their food supply.	You can save thousands every year growing your own vegetables.

Eliminate the Negative

There are a lot of problems involved in getting an A grade, but it's possible.	You, too, can get A's in school.
It's possible to build your own house; of course it can be difficult,	Yes, you can build your own house.

The Situation	Future Promise
and you will have to learn to handle many different problems and skills.	
These plans for putting together a canoe look difficult but I suppose anybody could actually do it.	Anybody can put this canoe together.
Living in this neighborhood can be difficult. There are some difficulties, however, mostly it's fun, but there's the noise, and once in a while some disputes.	It can be fun living in this neighborhood.

Future Promise—No Promise

Sometimes it's possible to make money by simply changing attitude.	A positive attitude can make you rich, but it's up to you.
Sometimes people have found that getting a raise. . . depends on them actually asking for it, if they don't nothing happens.	Getting a raise often is as easy as just asking for it.
Some people find they have talent and can write. . . magazines will pay money for good writing.	You can make money writing if you apply your talent.
Marriage can be difficult; primarily it depends on the individuals and whether they want a good marriage.	Marriage can be good if you're willing to work at it.

Any or all of these make up future promise. As you can see several of these are often automatically included. Anytime you utilize any one of these elements however you are utilizing future promise effectively.

HOW TO USE THE "I FACTOR" TO CREATE RESPONSE

Much earlier we mentioned talking directly to your reader. Now we want to cover it in more detail. The so-called "I factor" can cause tremendous reader response. Everybody likes to be recognized. Recognize someone and he will automatically identify with what you're saying. This can be done by inserting the word *you* and by showing the reader that you are thinking of his needs. If you say: *Our service department is being revamped and there will be some delay,* you will get very little sympathy or reaction from your reader. But what if you talk directly to him like this: *I'm sorry you had to wait so long for our service man to call. However, we've been revamping our service department to give you better service and he will get to you as quickly as possible.* This statement talks directly to him and shows him that what you're saying is to his advantage. Therefore, you will certainly get more cooperation than with almost any other approach.

Now let's try another one: *The company recently put in a new ruling that all lunches should be eaten in the lunchroom. Every employee will recognize that this will make our schedule more convenient for the company.* You're not liable to get any cooperation that way. So let's put the rule into effect: talk directly to the employee and sympathize with him.

We know you have been inconvenienced by the over-crowding in the lunchroom. Because of this we have initiated a new lunchroom schedule. If you will follow it we are sure that you will find lunchtime much pleasanter.

George Cranson, a company office manager, was in the habit of putting out three to four memo directives every week for his employees on such things as how to handle incoming letters, how to handle invoices, etc. The problem was that nobody paid any attention to the memos and office efficiency was extremely poor.

Fed up with this, George decided to try giving his employees a reason for his action in every memo from then on and to talk directly to them using the word *you.* His first memo explained why it was necessary to cut the coffee break back from 20 to 15 minutes and talked directly to the employees in terms of their benefits. The second explained why they should not park in the front parking lot, but in the back. Again the memo talked directly to the employees themselves. The response was immediate and over 90 percent of George's employees cooperated completely. From then on George employed this technique with every memo written. At the end of the year office efficiency was up a good 70 percent and George's office was considered the best in the company.

Now try it yourself and see if you can put the "I factor" in the sentences on the left.

Sentence	With the "I Factor" Added
In this age of heat 'n' serve convenience products, boxed dinners,	In this age of heat 'n' serve convenience products, boxed dinners,

Sentence	With the "I Factor" Added
and mass produced food, many homemakers are seeking more self expression.	and mass produced food, we know that you as a homemaker are looking for more self expression. . .
We have been requested to forward the enclosed proxy material relative to shares. The shares appear in the records of the company as . . .	This is important to you. We have been requested to send you the enclosed proxy material relative to the shares carried in your account.
Notice is hereby given that the annual meeting of the Thomas Corporation will be held at the company office at . . .	We want to inform you that the annual meeting of the Thomas Corporation will be held at the company office at . . .
An exhibit of paintings by Bay area artist Peter Saul will be featured in the main Art Gallery.	You might be interested in the exhibit of paintings by Bay area artist Peter Saul which will be featured in the main art gallery.
These new press flannel slacks are some of the finest on the market and people who give them the wear test usually keep them.	I would personally like you to wear-test these exciting new flannel slacks for a week.

THINK IN TERMS OF THE OTHER PERSON'S NEEDS

The greatest response from a reader is always obtained by putting the writing in terms of his needs. People are funny, since they think about everything in terms of themselves and aren't inclined to do anything unless it benefits them in some way.

Sometimes, of course, they are more intensively interested in one type of thing than another, and it is these things that will cause the most reaction. What we must do to obtain a good reaction is to slant our writing to the need.

What is slanting? Slanting is something every one of us does all the time and consists primarily of telling people what they want to hear.

A child learns quickly to tell his mother about those things he's done that she will approve of and to hold back those things that will bring disapproval. A student does the same thing with his teacher. He reports on subjects that the teacher has an interest in and keeps away from subjects he knows the teacher will disapprove of. In addition, he quickly finds out the kind of answers a teacher wants to hear on a test. A man does the same thing with the boss. Anytime you prepare a report for the boss the way he wants it you are slanting that report for your boss. The reason you do this, of course, is that it creates a favorable impression and brings approval. This is what you must think of when you expect action.

Fortunately, the job becomes easier since we ordinarily aren't writing for everybody in general but for particular groups of people. A student does a report for teachers and these teachers have certain likes and dislikes in common. The same is true of almost any group—housewives, students, mechanics, salesmen, bosses, church people, businessmen, and everyone else. Each of these groups has common traits.

And when you're considering a letter to these people which will bring action you must know these traits. In the beginning you'll have better luck if you write them down. For instance, say you're writing a letter to a group of housewives in which you want to get them together for a meeting to help protest some action in the community.

The first thing to do, either on paper or mentally, is to consider the common traits of housewives. List a few of them:

1) They have a husband and families.
2) Many are interested in homemaking.
3) They are vitally concerned with their children.
4) Many are home all day long.
5) Some work and have little time.
6) Most would welcome something to do during the day.

So if you were writing a letter to invite these people to a meeting you would have better luck in getting the housewives there if you would direct your appeal to these interests, the more the better. Let's try one.

Dear . . .

All of you know of the danger to our children from the trucks that are now being allowed to pass through the neighborhood. Together it's possible we might stop this.

Since many of you are free in the afternoon before the kids come home from school, why not join us at 1:00 at my house and we'll see what we can do about making the neighborhood safe again.

> If you work and can't make it give me a ring and at least let me know you support us.

You have now appealed to the mother's interest in the child's safety, to the fact that she has free time, and to any working mothers.

Undoubtedly, you will get some action. Naturally, the more intense you can make these appeals without overdoing it the better. (See the examples, Figures 1, 2, and 3, pp. 156-157.)

In this case, appealing to the group's needs was simple. Sometimes, however, it isn't that easy, yet the more important the action is to you the more work you will have to do to assure you're meeting those needs. When the action is extremely important—and is directed to an individual, a group, or particular company, then you will need to do some work. (Figures 4 and 5.)

For instance, Benton Hamilton, a teacher who had some background in selling, decided to get out of teaching and find a job in sales with a large company. The first thing he did was to go to the library and look up everything he could find on that company in *Fortune* and *Business Week*. He learned that while they were strong in selling to urban groups, they were weak with the farm and rural areas, and yet wanted to crack this market. They had in fact been spending considerable time trying to sell in that area.

He himself had had a farm and small town background and knew the rural people well. So in his initial letter Benton simply told them that he understood their needs and also had heard that they were especially interested in trying to crack the small town and farm market. He went on to state that this was his specialty. He had grown up on a farm, knew small town people, and knew that they bought from people who thought like they did and could become their friends. He had done some selling to this group, and had been successful. Therefore he felt that he could help them open up a territory that they probably couldn't open any other way.

This letter brought an immediate response from the personnel director, and although some of his qualifications were not what they wanted, they hired him anyway to meet this special need.

Not every group will need this kind of intensive look at their problems, but when it's important do some checking on their needs before you sit down to write. The key to action is reader's needs. Don't fake, but if you can offer those things that a reader wants then your chance of getting some action from him will be greatly increased.

Try thinking of traits that are common to the following groups on the left.

Groups	Traits, Likes, Activities, etc.
Farmers	hard working
	live in rural areas
	interest in farming etc.
	work close to the soil
	keep one eye on the weather
High school girls	boys
	school activities
	go to school
	clothes
	studies
	parents
Workers	their job
	the pay check
	working conditions
	after work activities
	their families
Skiers	ski equipment
	snow conditions
	resorts in the area
	the weather
	the outdoors
Car salesmen	making sales
	clothes
	money
	condition of the car market
	people's needs as they relate to sales

In this chapter you have again picked up an additional word power tool that will both improve your writing tremendously and make tremendous differences in everyday contacts with people. Thinking in terms of the other person's needs as outlined in this chapter every time you want somebody else to do something for you, you will not only get action immediately but will achieve results that will literally amaze you.

IN CONCLUSION

Many times we write to get some action. This, however, happens when the reader is motivated. We can increase reader motivation by offering future promise, by utilizing the "I factor," and by thinking in terms of the other person's needs.

Future Promise

The future holds excitement to most people, and often they will respond if you promise them something in the future. Here are the factors that make up future promise:

Talk of Tomorrow—To utilize this factor, talk of what your reader is going to receive in the future—education, health, etc.

Create an Illusion—Try, when possible, to create the illusion that whatever is promised is as good as accomplished.

Eliminate the Negative—Try, when utilizing future promise, to always stress the positive and simply ignore the negative.

Future Promise, No Promise At All—Good future promise promises the reader something he gets only by his own action. That is, the fulfillment of the promise is dependent on the reader.

Utilize the "I factor": Whenever possible, talk directly to your reader and try to think of his needs. This helps create response.

Think in Terms of the Other Person's Needs: The greatest response can be obtained by putting your writing in terms of the other person's needs. Fortunately, you don't ordinarily have to appeal to one person, but can "slant" to a group of people. Each of these groups has a number of traits in common. To achieve action consider these traits and write directly to them.

EXAMPLES OF WRITING THAT CONSIDERS THE OTHER PERSON'S NEEDS AND UTILIZES COMMON TRAIT APPEAL

Figure 1

Dear _____,

Good News!

Now we have a chance to do something about those taxes that are *affecting each and everyone* of us.

The Board of Supervisors has agreed to hold an additional meeting for the *area homeowners* and listen to arguments as to why they should not increase property taxes.

As you know, each of us who *owns a home and pays taxes* could come up with a dozen reasons.

Please be at the Harmer Building at 8:00 pm and help get these new taxes set aside.

("I factor" and trait appeal are both used.)

Figure 2

Dear _____,

What would you do if *your son* came to you and confessed that he had a drug problem? Naturally you'd help. But in this city there's nowhere to turn—*your minister, the police, your lawyer, a psychiatrist*—none of them has enough information to help.

Now we want to try to establish an organization that's equipped to help both *your child and mine* if they run into this kind of trouble and others.

Won't you come to a meeting Tuesday night, November 6, 8 pm, at the San Soma School and help us discuss the problem?

Figure 3

An Ad

What a delight to behold as you *scamper in your bath*. A birch front cabinet *finished by you* with a grain-revealing stain or a paint in a happy tone. A classically styled cabinet enhanced by the one-piece, marblelike top you've chosen in white and gold, or a *uniquely you* pastel. A graceful vanity to brighten *your* every morning's mood.

(This contains good "I factor" and appeals to several group traits—in italics.)

INTENSIVE RESEARCHED WRITING DIRECTED TO THE READER'S NEEDS

Figure 4

Dear_____,

Before requesting an interview for the position you have open, I took the liberty to find out exactly what your firm does, and noticed that you handle the accounts of a number of cafeterias. This is right down my line. In addition to being an accountant for five years, I was formerly a cafeteria manager and understand their problems and the problems you'll have in handling their accounts.

I think I can do a good job for you because I understand the needs thoroughly. Can I come in and talk about this position?

Figure 5

Dear_____,

You have been inclined not to help us in opposing the new community organization, but I have taken the time to thoroughly read the new proposal and here's how it applies to you directly.

They propose to let horses utilize the trail which runs 20 feet from your property line, put in a large, 80-foot-high tank within 30 feet of your front door, and fence off your front yard from the street on a strip of property which the entire community owns.

As you can see, you have a great deal to lose. I hope you will reconsider and join us Tuesday night.

Figure 6: Stiff Memo

We have been considering the results from your department and would like your opinion of whether or not a meeting of the entire department might not be a good idea. Here we can go over the entire department results for the week. Sometimes meetings like these get many diverse opinions which help pinpoint the problems and often result in suggestions which we are later able to work up into positive results.

Figure 7: Revised Memo

We are sure you want to bring your department's production record up. What we're considering is holding weekly meetings to review the week's problems and get suggestions for improvement. From this we hope to obtain positive ways to improve results. Let me know what you think of this idea.

11

How to Make Brashness Pay Off

Naturally, you won't use the quality of brashness in every piece of writing. It just isn't appropriate. But sometimes when you really want to produce results brashness can do the job for you when nothing else will. It's so extraordinary and outrageous that it makes the reader sympathize almost immediately. He says inwardly to himself, "Gosh if he'll go to that amount of trouble, I can at least do my part."

One famous example was the boy who went to apply for a job and found a tremendous line ahead of him. Now, he could have simply waited his turn like the other applicants. By that time, however, the interviewer would have seen so many others that his own application just wouldn't have stood out. And the odds against his getting the job would have been tremendous. What he needed was an *attention getter*. That's when he decided to be brash. After all, he had nothing to lose. So he left for a few minutes, and sent the interviewer a telegram.

It said simply: *Please don't give the job to anybody else until you've talked to freckle-faced Mike at the end of the line.* This added a brash sit-up twist the interviewer wasn't expecting. It caught his imagination and he called Mike in immediately.

There are other ways to do this. For instance, you send your employees a memo and it says: *Any man who can't quote every line of this memo to me will be transferred to another office.* Pretty brash, isn't it? But I'll bet they'll remember the memo, not because they're afraid of being transferred but because you really caught their attention.

You can do it in many other ways. Here's another letter: *I have been searching for an employer that is worthy of my intense know-how, loyalty, and merry disposition. May I come and see you?* It has a certain quality to it. It may not get the job, but it will be remembered.

Now let's look at some of the ingredients that go into making up this kind of brashness.

The Unexpected

A major quality of brashness on paper is that it's unexpected. How do you do this? If you want action, simply ask yourself what the person who's going to get that particular piece of writing expects. Then try to decide what you could say to him that would be completely unexpected.

For instance, if you intend to write a memo to get the men to put tools away, they're expecting one which will tell them why they should put tools away and how. They've seen a hundred of them. But they certainly aren't expecting a memo which says: *The next man to put a tool back will be fined $100.* That's startling. Of course you have to go on from there and turn it around. But it's certainly going to shake them up.

For instance, a note to a manufacturer complaining about a problem with a washing machine might start out by saying: *My new washing machine is being shipped to your office C.O.D.* It isn't but it will get his attention.

Or you might start off a sales memo by saying: *I don't have any idea whether you need this item or not, but it's already on its way to you.*

Or to a potential client you could say: *Don't buy anything else until you've talked to me.*

All of these things are unexpected and will cause a reaction. Basically, you simply want to startle him to the point where he'll give the rest of your message a real chance to get through.

Janice Gartner, a telephone company employee who sold real estate on weekends, needed some sort of a letter which would allow her, in a very limited amount of time, to pick up as many listings as possible. She wasn't quite sure what to expect, but she wrote a letter (mailed to homeowners at random) which started: *If you're ready to sell your house you really need me on your side because I'll work harder for you than anybody else I know.* She then mailed them out with a great deal of apprehension. The next day nothing happened, but the following day the phone practically rang off the hook, 180 people came into the office to see her, and several real estate agents called to complain that they had received a number of phone calls from their listings asking why that agent wasn't willing to work as hard for them as Janice was. From then on every letter of this type Janice sent out contained some type of brashness.

Now see if you can take these common place things and make them unexpected.

The Situation	The Unexpected
You're writing an important ad you want everyone to read.	Don't read this ad!
A classified ad to rent a house that you want to stand out.	This house is not for you.
You're writing a letter to customers asking them to renew their appliance warranty policy with you.	It's ridiculous to protect your appliances. Right?
You're writing a memo to your salesmen asking them to hold down their expense accounts.	How would you like to buy a brand new car and put it on your expense account?
Answering an ad for a secretary.	I'm the only secretary for you, and you'd better believe it.
A note to your child's principal complaining about a teacher's treatment.	Why not fire your teachers and let the janitors teach?

Be Outrageous

It never hurts to ask for something that you can't have. If you can't have it anyway you haven't really lost anything. Actually you've gained a couple of things. You've caught that person's attention and you've planted the idea in his mind that you're somebody who really goes after what he wants. For instance, you're a salesman and you're writing a follow-up. You say: *I want to sell you this car and every car you'll ever buy from now on.* Now you know that's almost impossible, but it establishes an image that many people respond to, especially when you go on to explain why in a logical manner. You might, for instance, say in your note to the shop: *I never want to see another tool out of place in here.*

Simply pick out an impossibility that applies to what you want to say and ask for it.

Now let's try it. Look at the situation on the left, and try to ask for something that's absolutely outrageous.

Common Place Idea	Outrageous Approach
You're applying for a job.	I expect you to stop interviewing right now and hold that job for me.
A note to your child's principal complaining about a teacher's treatment.	I expect you to reverse that teacher's grade and give my child an A.
A letter asking people to bring their cars into your gas station.	Don't put another gallon of gas in your car until you've talked to us.
A letter to the neighborhood calling a meeting to complain about a problem.	Come and help us to drive the proposed gas station right out of the neighborhood.
A note asking someone for money they owe you.	Don't make me write you again.
A letter to the school board.	I want to ask all of you to resign.

"Being outrageous" on paper sometimes can be interchanged with "saying the unexpected" because anything that is outrageous generally has to be unexpected. But the reverse isn't always true. In addition, an outrageous statement usually must be balanced by an explanation which makes it rational. Otherwise it has little credence. Whether you leave it extremely outrageous or only partially so depends on your audience.

Invent New Combinations

In doing the unexpected or the outrageous, try when possible to create new combinations. Try not to get into the rut of doing the same old thing all the time or of using ideas that will soon grow stale. How do you do this? Simply by using combinations that ordinarily don't go together. You might, for instance, jot down the following items: elephants, peanut butter, cars, thumbtacks, people, jelly, mountains, maraschino cherries, ants, bubble gum, and anything else you can think of—you'll create a word power tool that's extremely effective. Then when you start to write, pick the most unusual combinations you can think of on your list. For instance, how about ants and bubble gum. You might start off your note by saying: *It's gotten to the point where I don't expect this job to be finished until ants start chewing bubble gum.* And we both know that's going to be never. So...

Or you might pick out one of the others and say: *Getting action out of this company is much like trying to smear peanut butter on an elephant—fact is, it's impossible.*

As you can see, from any good list, either written or mental, you can create all sorts of wild and very unexpected word power combinations that your reader just isn't going to see coming. And that's what you're trying to do.

Now take the items from the list below and see if you can make unusual combinations from the rather commonplace situations. When finished compare them to the combinations we've created:

custard pie	boats
wall.	babies
mice	hands
Scotch tape	ocean
wallpaper	peanut
trailers	piano
roller skate	nickel

You create a word power tool that's extremely effective. Many people have achieved startling results using this word power tool. In one case, Marty Gordon was having trouble getting his child into a school out of district. He tried talking to the people in the office several times without results and failed in his attempt to get an appointment with the principal. Finally he sat down and wrote a letter. In it he got extremely wild, comparing the job of getting through the office staff to the job of trying to cross the Great Wall of China. He finished by making the point that he would roller skate around the world, sit on top of the school flagpole, or lower himself down the side of the building by a rope if the principal would only see him. Marty mailed it off without much hope. Much to his surprise he got a call from the principal two days later and within a week had permission to change his child's school—all because he thought he didn't have a chance and decided to get *really outrageous*.

Common Situation	Unusual Combinations
You're applying for a job.	Sometimes trying to find the right man for your company is much like trying to pin a custard pie to the wall.
A note to your child's principal complaining about a teacher's treatment.	What I've found is that trying to communicate with this teacher is almost like trying to push a peanut up a mountain. . . In other words, it's almost impossible.
A letter asking people to bring their car into your gas station.	We don't really care how you get here, ride a roller skate, take a trailer, come mouseback. . .but whatever you do don't miss getting into Don's Service Station during give-away days.
A note asking a friend for money that he owes you.	I know you'd roller skate across the ocean if I'd asked; however, I'll make it easier. All I want this time is . . .
A letter to the neighborhood calling a meeting to complain about a problem.	Individual complaints sometimes have about as much effect as trying to pull a trailer with a piece of Scotch tape . . together, however. . .

Assume That It's True

One of the most refreshing things is ignorance. People constantly hem in what they're doing with all sorts of qualifications—often making it almost impossible to get anything done. You've heard people say well, I'd like to do this, but there's this, and this, and this, and this.

In being brash, you've got to at times be ignorant. Even if you know all of the problems, or qualifications, ignore them. Simply act as though they didn't exist. This will not only startle your reader, but sometimes it will also get him to say: *Why, yes, it is just as simple as that.*

Certainly you have seen people in everyday life who simply ignore the problems and step in and get the job done. Sometimes you can't worry about offending other people, about trespassing on rights, about stepping on toes, or about breaking rules. You've got to just ignore it and write as if what you want is going to happen and it's going to happen immediately.

For instance, someone's been dragging their feet on getting some information for you, so you write them and say: *Thanks for your note. I know you're working on the problem, and I'll be in tomorrow morning bright and early to get the information.* Now he hasn't got it but chances are he's going to break his back to do something if he knows you're coming in expecting it. Or you might say to a company that you know takes a long time in getting orders out. *We're running an ad advertising your product one week from today. If you can get the merchandise to us by Wednesday we'll have the chance to set up a large display before the ad runs.*

Now you might not get any action from this, but if it gets to the right person it puts the pressure on. This technique cannot be used at all times, but sometimes it's necessary to simply ignore and to state it like you know it's going to happen.

See if you can write a sentence *assuming that it's true* for the situation on the left.

The Situation	Assuming That It's True
You're applying for a job.	I'm not sure I can go to work this week but I can probably report by next Monday.
A note to your child's principal complaining about a teacher's treatment.	I'll be in Wednesday and I'm sure you'll have the problem taken care of by that time.
A letter asking people to bring their car into your gas station.	We know you're going to come in. After all, who else does the job we do?
A note asking a friend for money that they owe you.	I'll meet you Wednesday and you can give me the cash.
A letter to the neighborhood calling a meeting to complain about a common problem.	And there's no doubt we're going to get this situation corrected.

Be Sold on What You're Saying

Brashness only works well if you're really convinced. Therefore, when you're going to use brashness on paper as a word power tool, be convinced that what you're saying or asking for is really best and is really important. If it's you you're selling, have complete faith in yourself, and be as brash as possible. You're writing a letter to get a job so instead of saying, *I'm answering your ad for a secretary,* you say: *How would you like to have a secretary that will double your office production? What office wouldn't? I don't think I'm bragging at all when I say I can do just this. I've specialized in getting an office running efficiently over nine years now and I can do a superior job. Of course the proof is in actually doing it. So why don't I come in and give you a sample of what I mean?*

This is a good example of being sold on yourself. Pick out that trait which you really have confidence in and then be brash about it, don't pull any punches, and state it in a dramatic overblown way.

When You Have an Idea, Try It!

In trying to be brash, it's important not to discard ideas just because they're "way out." If you get an idea that you think might work, even though it 'might seem crazy, try it. It might be the best idea you ever had.

For instance, the idea of Mike's to send a telegram saying, *Wait until you've seen freckle-faced Mike at the end of the line,* might have seemed silly, but as a result he got immediate attention. Therefore if you can think of it, *try it.*

For instance, you're about to write a letter answering an ad for a job in selling. Now you know that the company wants more money and you want more money and somehow if you can combine them in a startling approach it might be interesting. So you try to tie those two ideas together like this: *This is a letter asking for more money. You don't know me and that's not important. I want more money than I'm now making and I think that with your product I can not only make more money for me but for you, too. I've got several ideas along this line that I'd like to talk to you about.* This, then, makes a fairly unusual letter that probably would get a response. It employs brashness, confidence, and took an idea that you'd normally reject and made it work. No matter what kind of writing it is, if you can think of it, if it seems pretty reasonable to you, and if you can tie it together with the other person's needs, then try it. You may have to work with six or seven or even twenty drafts to make it work, but try it. You may come up with better results than you ever expected.

Go Directly to the Person That Can Make It Happen

Brashness will do you no good at all if it doesn't get to the person who can do something about it. A letter asking for a job interview that gets only to the secretary or some subordinate probably won't do you any good. Therefore, try to decide who has the authority to take the action you want and then send that directly to them. It might be the manager of the company, it might be your boss, it might be a foreman, it might be a doctor, it might be almost anybody depending on what you're writing. But you'll get far better action if your piece of writing gets to the person who can do something about it.

Clements Zieger, an office manager with a small Dallas company, tried in vain to get one of the company's shop tools repaired by the manufacturer. He wrote eight letters and even called the company three times. His calls were shunted to somebody who said he'd take care of the complaint but nothing ever happened. Finally, Clements got really mad, looked up the name of the president from some of the company literature, and wrote a blistering letter to him which started by saying: *I don't know if you realize that somebody in your company is undermining your company's good reputation, but I thought you might like to be told about it.* The letter went out one morning, the next afternoon he received a call from the president himself. He wanted to know all about it, and had already sent a crew out from the plant to repair the machine. Finally, he told Clements if anything like this ever happened again he was to call him directly.

You now have a good general idea of what Word Power Dynamics is, and how to make it work for you effectively. The word power approach as you can see is different and unique. Other books teach English or how to write, but only this one teaches Word Power Dynamics. From now on, whenever you have a problem either in writing or in everyday life where you feel one of these word power principles can help, you should turn to that chapter and go over it again in detail. As you improve your writing and learn how to make word power really work for you, you'll probably want to come back from time to time to make sure you're applying the principles effectively.

The final chapter of this book will show you how to take all the word principles covered throughout, and put them together for effective use in every type of writing.

12

How
to Apply Word Power
to All Kinds of Writing

Now that you understand what Word Power Dynamics is all about, how do you go about using this information? How do you apply the word power principles to a memo from the boss to his employees, a letter answering a help wanted ad, a selling letter, a pamphlet, a report, and other kinds of written communication?

In general, what you need to know is what audience you're writing for (that is whether you should be formal or informal), and whether or not you need to sell your reader or simply communicate with him.

For instance, if you're writing a letter to a business or the president of a company, you'll be more formal in your tone than you will if you're writing a letter to the workers in the back shop or to someone you know well.

In addition, the more need you have to sell somebody on something, as in a letter answering a help wanted ad or a sales letter, the more emotional elements you will need, such as image projection, attention to the other person's need, etc.

HOW TO DECIDE ON THE ELEMENTS YOU'LL NEED

It's very simple to decide what should go in a particular piece of writing. All you need are the guides given in this chapter: the

Audience Type Guide (Figure 1), the Need Type Guide (Figure 2), the Utilization Guide (Figure 3), and the Communication Elements Rating Scale (Figure 4).

To use them, first decide what audience type you're trying to write to (Figure 1). If it's a personal note, this will be *talky;* if it's a communication to a business such as a business letter, this will be *semiformal,* etc. Next, try to decide what you need to do (Figure 2). Are you simply going to get a message across, such as in a memo? Do you need to show someone why they should do something, like trying to get a group out to a meeting? Or do you need to hard sell, like in some types of direct mail pieces?

Now take a look at the Utilization Guide (Figure 3) and it will tell you which elements you should include and in about what degree.

Let's take an example. You're writing a letter to invite some friends to a meeting. The Audience Type Guide (Figure 1) says this should be *conversational.* In addition, since you must give them a reason for coming, you'll want to rate it on the Need Guide (Figure 2) as *establishing a need.* Now if you'll look on the Utilization Guide (Figure 3) under *Establishing a Need, Conversational,* you'll find that this piece of writing should have a readability index of 5, a conversational tone of 5, be tight and come to the point fairly well, have a fairly good ho-hum crasher, get attention, etc.

Simply go down each element seeing how it rates. This will give you an idea what you need to put in your own writing. Next, write the piece, then come back and rate what you've done on the Communication Elements Rating Scale (Figure 4). Finally, compare it on the Utilization Guide (Figure 3).

If, for instance, yours rates 0 in coming to the point, and it should rate from 3 to 5, then you've got to do some revision. If your writing rates 0 for tightness, and it should rate 5, then you've got to revise it. The same holds true for all other elements. Once you've decided who your audience is and what you're trying to do, it's simple to tell whether you've done a good job or not. If you haven't just revise those elements that need extra work.

Now, let's use the four guides in this chapter (Figures 1, 2, 3, and 4), to decide which word power elements belong in different kinds of writing. After doing this, in most cases, I have revised each piece of written communication to utilize the word power principles as effectively as possible.

Figure 1

AUDIENCE GUIDE

Audience Type

Formal	Scientific papers, formal communications to business.
Semiformal	Communications to business—some news, releases, some memos; letters from business to customers; pamphlets; etc.
Conversational	Most memos; most sales letters; announcement letters—letters asking for a job; some letters to businesses and between businesses.
Talky	Personal notes—memos to friends, etc. (This type will not be included in the Utilization Guide.)

Figure 2

NEED GUIDE

Need Type

Communication	The need is simply to get the message across. Little need to establish the reason for doing something or to sell your reader.
Semi-need	Communication is of primary importance, but you'll get more cooperation if your reader understands. Memos, some kinds of brochures and pamphlets.
Establishing a Need	It is necessary to establish the importance of the subject. Good image projection important. Can sometimes use motivation.
Sales Material	The primary need is to sell your reader. Usually has image, emotion, and motivation, sometimes brashness.
Hard Sell	Primarily, need to hard sell. Strong on emotion and motivation.

Figure 3

UTILIZATION GUIDE

To use, decide which audience and need type you have for your particular piece of writing. Follow that need type down through each word power element. The guide will tell you whether or not you need a particular element and in what quantity.

Need Types Word Power Elements	Commun-ication	Semi-need	Establish a need	Sales material	Hard sell	Audience types
Readability index	3 3-5 5	3 3-5 5	3 5 5	3 5 5	3 5 5	Formula Semiformal Conversational
Conversational tone	3 3-5 5	3 3-5 5	3 3-5 5	3 3-5 5	3 3-5 5	Formal Semiformal Conversational
Come to the Point			all 3-5			Formal Semiformal Conversational
Tight Writing			all 5			Formal Semiformal Conversational
Ho-Hum Crasher	0-3 0-3 0-3	3 3 3	3 3-5 3-5	3-5 3-5 3-5	3-5 3-5 3-5	Formal Semiformal Conversational
Attention Getting Elements	0-5 0-5 0-5	0-5 0-5 0-5	3 3 3	3 3 3	3 3 3	Formal Semiformal Conversational
Goals			all 3-5			Formal Semiformal Conversational

Need Types / Word Power Elements	Commun-ication	Semi-need	Establish a need	Sales material	Hard sell	Audience types
Logical Organization or impact formula			all 3-5			Formal Semiformal Conversational
Image projection	*See explanation for differences		all 3-5			Formal Semiformal Conversational
Emotional Goals			all 3-5			Formal Semiformal Conversational
Earns appeal	0 0 0-3	0 0 0-3	0 0-3 0-5	2 3 3-5	2 3 3-5	Formal Semiformal Conversational
Future Promise	0 0 0	0 0-3 0-3	0-3 3 3	2-3 3-5 3-5	2-3 3-5 3-5	Formal Semiformal Conversational
" I Factor"	0-3 0-5 0-5	0-3 0-5 0-5	0-3 3-5 0-5	0-3 3-5 3-5	0-3 3-5 3-5	Formal Semiformal Conversational
Other person's needs		0-2 2 2-3	2-4 2-4 2-5	3-5 3-5 3-5	3-5 3-5 5	Formal Semiformal Conversational
Brashness				0-5 0-5 0-5	0-5 0-5 0-5	Formal Semiformal Conversational

* Writing which primarily needs to communicate (most memos, some letters, etc.) should simply use only basic words for image projection (not the other image projection elements).

* Longer types of communication (reports, pamphlets, technical papers, etc.) are classified under semi-need. In this type of writing you often need to establish why what you're writing about is important, or to explain basic points in some detail. The more it's necessary to do this, the more you should use the other image producing elements: examples, projected word pictures, etc.

* The more you need to sell (selling letters, advertising, etc.), the more you will want to use symbols and emotion.

* The "I factor" is used when it's necessary to talk directly to your reader. This is always the preferred form. However, certain kinds of communication (news releases, some brochures, reports, etc.) use the third person.

* Brashness is used when the odds are against you, or when you need to get the other person's attention. Don't use this element unless you have a good reason.

Figure 4

COMMUNICATION ELEMENTS—RATING SCALE

1. *Readability Index* (See Chapter 2)

How well a piece of writing communicates depends primarily on its readability index rating.

(Remember to find the readability index, count the number of sentences in a 100 word sample, and divide this into 100. This gives you the average number of words per sentence. Then count the words in the 100 word sample with over seven letters per word. Add these two together and divide by two.) Now here's how that rates on the word power scale:

Readability Index	Word Power Rating
23 plus	0
17 to 20 or 10–12	3
13 to 15	5

2. *Conversational Talk* (See Chapter 2)

Here are examples to compare against:

Plain Talk Sentences	Word Power Rating
The decontamination of the ingredients through the maximizing of all the elements available results in. . .	0
It's not getting much better because in many ways the situation is acute, for instance, this very question. . .	3
What all these theories boil down to is getting more work with less effort and you want to make the man himself say: why did I work so darn hard in the first place?	5

Rate your own writing by comparing it against the examples on the left. If it's in-between, give it an in-between rating—1, 2, or 4.

3. *Come to the Point* (See Chapter 2)

Never coming to the point rates 0, coming to the point immediately rates 5.

Example	Word Power Rating
When the safety contest ended it was some time before the company announced that they had come to a decision. Even then they didn't announce the name of the winners but waited another three weeks before saying anything. There was a lot of talk at that time about actually cancelling the contest altogether but an employee committee talked the president into it. I think Bill James, Tom Jordan and Mary Halverson finally won.	0
It took three weeks after the first announcement before the winners of the company safety contest were	3

Example	*Word Power Rating*
named. *The final winners were Bill James, Tom Jordan, and Mary Halverson. At one time there was some talk of cancelling but an employee committee talked the company president into it.*	
Bill James, Tom Jordan and Mary Halverson finally won the company safety contest.	5

Since there are many types of writing let's give you another example here:

Example

It is difficult to put the Easy Master table together unless you have the proper light. The box looks like it doesn't contain enough parts but it does. If you will follow the instructions on page 4 it will go together easily.	0
The Easy Master package contains all the parts you will need for easy assemblage. To put your Easy Master table together, simply follow the instructions on page 4.	3
To put your Easy Master table together follow the instructions on page 4. The package contains all the parts you will need for easy assembly.	5

4. *Tight Writing:* (See Chapter 2)

Writing in addition to the other elements should get your message across in the fewest number of words possible. Here's the gauge:

Writing rambles	0
Reasonably tight	3
Extremely tight	5

5.*Impact* (See Chapter 3)

Try to use the impact elements in all writing, but since most are rated in other areas we will not detail them here.

6. *Sludge* (See Chapter 4)

Sludge can be effectively measured under both the readability index and conversational talk. Extremely sludged writing for instance will show up on the readability index as 26 plus. Conversely unsludged writing will give an acceptable index. This element will not be rated here.

Attention Commanding Elements

1. *Ho-Hum Crasher* (See Chapter 5)

An opening that doesn't grab the reader rates 0, one that catches the reader promptly 5.

Examples

In a previous letter to you we stressed the importance of properly conducting your account and asked your coopera-tion in refraining from drawing checks for insufficient funds.	0
We ask your cooperation in refraining from drawing checks against in-sufficient funds.	3
Do you know what happened to your checking account this time?	5

Good Ho-Hum crashers using direct address, promise, and the Gee Whiz approach, would also rate 5.

2. *Other Attention Getting Elements* (See Chapter 5)

This consists of telling your reader what to expect, guideposts, novelties, questions, and answers, short sentences, dialogue, and word excitement. Rate any use of these items 3 points, more than one use 5 points.

3. *Goals* (See Chapter 6)

Every piece of writing with little apparent purpose rates 0, those with purpose, but not evident in every paragraph rates 3, writing where the purpose is clear in every paragraph rates **5.**

4. *Organization* (See Chapter 7)

Use either the logical organization or the impact formula.

Logical Organization (See Chapter 7)

Writing which rambles. The organization is not clear.	0
Writing where one point follows another with reasonable logic, yet discusses the same thing in several places, organization not quite clear.	3
Writing where the writer starts with a point that is developed logically from one end to the other. And the structure can be seen clearly.	5

Impact Formula (See Chapter 7)

Here are the elements:

Hey There
See Here
For Example
What's Up
So What

Each of these not developed, rate 0. Each fully developed rates 2.

5. *Image Projector* (See Chapter 8)

You can turn words and ideas into pictures, you can use comparisons, symbols and projected moving pictures. You can also get rid of collapsed words. Every time you use good picture elements, etc. give yourself 5 points, 3 points for some use, for every collapsed word take off 2 points.

6. *Emotion* (See Chapter 9)

Look at the piece of writing and decide what your emotional goal was. Then check some of the words at random, and try to decide if the emotional effect you want to achieve is actually the one you are achieving.

Doesn't correspond at all	0
Partially corresponds	3
If emotions correspond with the goal	5

Emotional Appeals

No inclusion	0
If you have alluded to it	3

Emotional Appeals

If you have included one of the four
Emotional Appeals—money

                preservation

                romance

                recognition   5

Motivation (See Chapter 10)

Motivation included future promise, the "I factor," and the other person's needs.

1. *Future Promise*

Future promise consists of talking of tomorrow, creating an allusion, eliminating the negative and making the promise contingent on the other person doing something. Give yourself 5 points each time you use good future promise, 2 points for vague future promise.

2. *"I Factor"*

Talk indirectly to your reader (third person, etc.)	0
Talk to the reader part of the time but use impersonal language.	3
Talk to your reader about his needs all the way through.	5

3. *Other Person's Needs*

Try to decide on the different traits your readers have in common and appeal to as many of those traits as possible.

No appeal	0
Appeal to two traits	3
Appeal to 3 or more traits	5

Brashness (see Chapter 11)

If your writing is direct and straight forward: 0
If it is extremely brash and outspoken: 5

LETTERS

Different kinds of letters have different requirements. Here's one written by an organization to one of its member chapters.

(The Original)

Dear_____,

According to the records of our accounting department, your chapter owes the amount listed below for the program indicated. We would appreciate your sending this amount now as we have already expended the funds necessary for the participation of your student in the BAL programs.

If there are circumstances which prevent your completing payment at this time, would you please let us know what your situation is and when you expect to be able to send the full amount.

We realize that your check may have crossed our letter in the mail. If this is the case, please disregard this letter.

Thank you for taking care of this matter.

Sincerely yours,

This letter not only needs to communicate, but it also needs to more or less establish a need. Since it is a letter from an organization to its chapters it can be either semiformal or conversational, depending on how you feel about it. Therefore, let's establish the need type as *Semi-Need* and the audience type as *Semiformal* (Figures 1 and 2). It should have a readability index of at least 3 (Figure 3), be fairly conversational, come to the point well, be tight, have a slight ho-hum crasher and some attention-getting elements. It should have good organization, use basic words for image projection, and pay at least slight attention to the other person's needs.

To see how it rates, see page 185.

The first letter, as you can see, rates low on the needed elements. Now let's revise it, concentrating on these points:

Readability

Conversational Tone

Coming to the Point

Tight Writing

A Ho-Hum Crasher
Organization
Basic Image Words
Other Person's Needs
An Explanation.

Word Power Scale Rating			
	Word power element ratings for a semi-formal audience and a Semi-Need need type taken from the Utilization Guide (Figure 3).	Rating of this letter on the Communication Elements Rating Scale (Figure 1).	Revision
Plain talk			
Readability index	3–5	2	5
Conversational tone	3–5	3	5
Comes to the point	3–5	3	5
Tight writing	5	4	5
Commands attention			
Ho-Hum crasher	3	0	4
Attention-getting elements	3–5		
Goals	3–5	5	5
Organization			
Logical	3–5	3	5
Impact Formula			
Image Projection	3–5	0	3
Emotion			
Emotional goal	3–5	3	3
Earns appeals	0	2	4
Motivation			
Future promise	0–3	0	0
"I factor"	0–5	4	5
Other person's needs	2	0	4
Brashness			
		28	53

(The Revision)

Dear_____,

This is a letter asking for money.

The program we billed you for is already underway and, naturally, we've spent the money on it to finance your student. For this reason we need this amount back from you.

Now, we know it's sometimes difficult for volunteer organizations to raise money, so let us know if you can pay this amount now.

If you can't, try to give us a possible payment date.

Cordially,

Since this letter is *Semi-Need* and as this organization needs something from its members, it must use a little explanation—correcting this and the other elements, including the other person's needs, this revision does a much better job.

Let's consider an announcement letter from a major company.

Dear_____,

A NEW BOOK
For the Do-It-Yourself Cook

In this age of heat 'n' serve convenience products, boxed dinners, and mass-produced food, many homemakers are seeking more self-expression and personal satisfaction in the kitchen. Helpful as these conveniences are, there comes a time when homemakers want to create a truly satisfying and delicious treat—and they want to do it themselves from start to finish.

Now Great Western introduces one of the most creative and innovative books for the do-it-yourself cook: *HOMEMADE BREAD COOK BOOK.* One way the homemaker can express herself and please family and friends is by serving her own freshly baked bread which, incidentally, is a very important staple food.

You see, together with cereal products, bread is one of the Basic Four Food Groups and is an important part of good, balanced nutrition. And *HOMEMADE BREAD COOK BOOK* can help fulfill the day's nutritional requirements with any one of its 185 delicious and nourishing recipes—from breakfast rolls to dessert breads.

And the cook will be especially happy to know that this 96 page book takes advantage of the latest preparation methods refined by yeast and flour manufacturers and includes a recent technique referred to as the "easy-mix" method. Plus—helpful tips, how-to photos, and easy-to-follow directions are included to help make bread baking easier.

On sale February 15, *HOMEMADE BREAD COOK BOOK* retails for only $1.95, so stock up now on this timely new book from Great Western.

Cordially,

This is a sales letter. The need type, then, is *Sales Material* (Need Guide, Figure 2), and the audience type is probably *Conversational* (the Audience Guide, Figure 1). This means the letter should have a readability index of 5 (Utilization Guide, Figure 3), be conversational, come to the point, be tight, have a fairly good ho-hum crasher, some attention getting elements, have good organization, give examples or create word pictures, include some emotional appeals, have some future promise, good "I factor," and good concentration on other person's needs. It doesn't, however, need brashness.

Let's rate it. (See page 188.)

Now let's look at it point by point.

There are four sentences per 100 words and 16 words over seven syllables for a readability index of 21 and a word power index of 1. The tone, however, is very conversational; it comes right to the point and uses no excess words. Therefore, the rating under plain talk is fairly high.

It hooks in reasonably well, and makes you want to read on to find out what the satisfaction is. It tells you what to expect in the second paragraph. It also follows the impact formula almost to the letter, like this:

Hey There: In this age of heat 'n' serve . . . homemakers are seeking more self-expression. . .

See Here: Homemakers want to create a truly satisfying and delicious treat . . . now Great Western introduces one of the most creative and innovative books. . .

For example: Bread is one of the basic four food groups . . . with its 185 delicious recipes (this is quite modified).

What's up: This 96 page book . . . includes the . . . easy mix
               method . . . plus . . . helpful tips. . .

So what: So stock up now. . :

Image: This book makes use of colorful image terms such as
               "easy mix method" . . . do it yourself cook . . . etc.
               This gives a clear picture of what's meant.

	Word power element ratings for a *Conversational* audience and a *Sales Material* need type taken from the Utilization Guide (Figure 3).	Rating of actual letter on the Communication Elements Rating Scale (Figure 1).
Plain talk		
Readability index	5	1
Conversational tone	5	4
Comes to the point	3-5	5
Tight writing	5	4
Commands attention		
Ho-hum crasher	3-5	4
Attention getting		
elements	3	1
Goals	3-5	3
Organization		
Logical		
Impact formula	3-5	5
Image projection	3-5	3
Emotion		
Emotional goal	3-5	3
Earns appeals	3-5	4
Motivation		
Future promise	3-5	3
"I factor"	3-5	2
Other person's needs	3-5	5
Brashness	0-5	—
		47

It uses emotion by appealing to preservation (foods) and self-recognition and expression. . .

It offers future promise and it appeals in several ways to homemakers' traits: do it yourself . . . express yourself . . . please family and friends, etc. . .

Except for the word index rating, this letter covers all of the elements well. And even though the index rating is low it still does a very good job.

Now let's consider a mail order sales letter. (See page 190.)

This is a letter from an organization trying to sell something to men by mail. The need type is definitely *Hard Sell* (Need Guide, Figure 2), and, by choice, the audience type is *Conversational* (Audience Guide, Figure 1). This means, then (considering Figure 3), the letter should have a readability index of 5, good conversational tone, may be almost talky, come to the point, be tight, have a good ho-hum crasher with attention getting elements, good organization, good image projection, good appeals, future promise, the "I factor," and other person's needs. Also, since this letter is going into people's homes and has to compete with many offers like this, it probably needs at least some brashness to get the job done.

For its rating, check page 191.

There are 20 words per sentence and eight words over seven syllables for a readability index of 14—word power rating 5.

This letter is very conversational, comes right to the point, and the writing is fairly tight, although some words could be eliminated without changing the meaning. Using direct address, it hooks in well.

It uses visual appearance well to capture attention.

It has a definite purpose, although it wanders a little by inserting a few too many details without tying it in.

Organization

It uses an impact formula like this:

Hey There: I would like you personally to . . .

See here: This is just my way of proving to you first-hand that these luxury flannels . . .

For example: Sharply creased that I personally guarantee new slacks free . . . The example portion can be extremely modified if it expands on the see here part.

Dear Mr. Jones:

I would like you to personally wear-test my exciting NEW "Blair-Press" Permanent Press Flannel Slacks for a week at my expense.

> That is why I'm sending two pairs of these luxury flannels to your Twin Rocks Rd. address.

There is no obligation for you to keep them. This is just my way of proving to you first-hand that these luxury flannels in stylish new checks, stripes, and solids not only look great, but will KEEP their first-on, just-pressed look throughout your longest days.

I am so sure my "Blair-Press" Permanent Press will keep this miracle Flannel* of Acrilan, rayon, and polyester looking neat and sharply creased that I personally guarantee *New Slacks Free* if these slacks ever lose their press!

When your two pairs arrive, put them to this test:

> Wear them hard. Toss them in your home washer. Dry them in your dryer or on a hanger. Then wear them again *Without Pressing.*

You'll be amazed! They look so perfect—smooth, neatly pressed, sharply creased—ready to wear anywhere with pride.

Please understand, Mr. Jones, when your slacks come, there is no obligation for you to keep them. You can return them after your week's free trial and owe nothing—not even an explanation!

They have all the styling and many of the "extras" that are found in $20 slacks.

But, a price that is not the $20 you'd expect. Only $17.95 for *two* pairs. That's just $8.97½ a pair!

Better send your order form today—they're sure to go fast.

Sincerely,

President

JLB/F

What's up: When your slacks come there is no obligation for you to keep them. You can return them.

So what: Better send your order form today ...

There are lots of symbolic word pictures—wear test, wear them hard, dry them in your dryer, sharply creased—and you can actually see these words.

Emotion

The writer here is attempting to create some excitement by the use of his words and he does fairly well at this. He includes both a money and a recognition appeal.

	Word power element ratings for a <u>Conver-ational</u> audience and a <u>Hard Sell</u> need type taken from the Utilization Guide (Figure 3).	Rating of actual direct mail sales letter on the Communication Elements Rating Scale (Figure 1).
Plain talk		
Readability index	5	5
Conversational tone	5	5
Comes to the point	3—5	5
Tight Writing	5	3
Commands attention		
Ho-hum crasher	3—5	4
Attention getting		
elements	3	2
Goals	3—5	3
Organization		
Logical		
Impact formula	3—5	3
Image projection	3—5	5
Emotion		
Emotional goal	3—5	4
Earns appeals	3—5	2
Motivation	3—5	5
Future promise	3—5	5
"I factor"		
Other person's needs	5	3
Brashness	0—5	5
		59

He motivates by future promise and utilizes the "I factor" extremely well, talking directly to the reader. He also utilizes the reader's desire to look good and to try something before buying it.

Brashness

This writer has been extremely brash here by stating that he's sending you two pairs of slacks. You certainly aren't expecting this.

It should be pointed out while this letter has a fairly high rating it certainly is not perfect. Anything above 35 points will communicate well. The fact that it has high points above this doesn't necessarily mean it's doing the job well. It just means it contains more elements. But, in addition to simply having them, you must make sure that the use of those elements is appropriate for your audience. A very familiar style wouldn't be appropriate for some audiences. Neither would too much brashness. It depends on what you're trying to do and who's going to read it. In this case, the writer probably is a little bit too gee-whiz with things like *exciting new slacks* etc., so that he begins to lose his authenticity. In addition, his organization is not perfect, since he wanders away from the main point a little too much to get in the details about the slacks: *Wear them hard. Toss them in your home washer. Dry them in your dryer or on a hanger. Then wear them again without pressing.* Those all hit hard and stand out. While this letter could certainly be improved by a softer sell, it's not too bad.

Let's consider a letter answering a help wanted ad. (See page 193.)

A letter answering a help wanted ad or applying for a job must of necessity be a selling letter. It must establish your qualification, as well as point out how you can help them with their special needs.

The need type is *Sales Matter* (Need Guide, Figure 2), the audience type can range from *Semiformal* to *Conversational* (*Semiformal* often works well.) Then, from Figure 3, the letter must have a readability index of 5, good conversational tone, must come to the point, be tight, have a fair ho-hum crasher and attention getting elements, good organization, some image getting elements, usually in the form of examples, offer emotional appeal, future promise, good "I factor," and cater to the person's needs. How much brashness you use depends on whether you think your reader will accept it, and how great the odds are against your getting the job.

The greater the odds, the more brashness you want to use.

Note how the letter rates. (See page 194.)

The first letter, as you can see, rates low on the needed points. Let's revise it, correcting the plain talk portion and a few other elements, and leaving out motivation and brashness.

Here are the elements corrected on page 195.

readability index

conversational tone

coming to the point

tight writing

attention getting

organization

image projection (basic words)

---

(1)

Last week, you advertised for a salesman in the *Bee*, for which I would like to inquire if it is still open. During the entire 15 years I have devoted in my life to selling, I have attempted to upgrade my approach to the field and to achieve the maximum of my ability. As a result, I sold appliances for five years sharpening my techniques, then tires, and finally moved to Doman Holdwan where I have had good success.

During my adult life (I am 38) I have been devoted to the community and have achieved some outstanding success in Kiwanis, Junior Chamber of Commerce, 20-30 Club, and others. I believe strongly in contributing to the community and have worked hard to do my part.

If we could talk I am sure you would feel I could do a good job for you.

References: Thomas J. Hans, Sales Manager, Doman Holdwan,
Will J. Horton, Manager, First National Bank

	Word power element ratings for a <u>Conver-sational</u> audience and a <u>Hard Sell</u> need type taken from the Utilization Guide (Figure 3).		Ratings of different letters on the Communication Elements Rating Scale (Figure 4)			
	Standard letter	Brash letter	(1)	(2)	(3)	(4)
Plain talk						
Readability index	5	5	0	3	5	5
Conversational tone	5	5	0	3	5	5
Comes to the point	3–5	3–5	0	4	4	4
Tight writing	5	5	2	5	5	5
Commands attention						
Ho-hum crasher	3–5	3–5	0	2	5	5
Attention getting elements	3	3	0	2	3	3
Goals	3–5	3–5	3	3	3	3
Organization						
Logical	3–5	3–5	5	5	5	5
Impact formula						
Image projection	3–5	3–5	0	3	4	4
Emotion						
Emotional goal	3–5	3–5	3	3	3	3
Earns appeals	3–5	3–5	0	2	5	5
Motivation						
Future promise	3–5	3–5	0	0	4	5
"I factor"	3–5	3–5	4	4	5	5
Other person's needs	3–5	3–5	0	0	3	5
Brashness	—	3–5	0	0	2	4
			17	39	61	65

---

(2)

I would like to apply for the position of salesman that you advertised in the *Sacramento Bee*.

I have had 15 years of sales experience–some in the appliance business, five years selling tires, and five years as senior salesman for Doman Holdwan. I believe I know selling from all standpoints.

I am 38 years old, married, and extremely active in community activities, having belonged to Kiwanis, Junior Chamber of Commerce, 20-30 Club, and a number of others.

Here are two references who will vouch for me:

References: Thomas J. Hans, Sales Manager, Doman Holdwan,
        Will J. Horton, Manager, First National Bank

May I have the opportunity to come and talk to you about this position?

This is a pretty typical letter. It's OK if you have good solid qualifications and there are few applicants for the job. But it doesn't do any motivating.

Let's do another increasing all elements and adding good emotional appeals, the "I factor," future promise, and the other person's needs.

---

(3)

Selling is a great field!

And one in which I have devoted my life. That's why your ad for a salesman in the *Sacramento Bee* intrigued me. I have had 15 years of sales experience–some in the appliance business, five years selling tires, and five years as senior salesman for Doman Holdwan. During my Doman Holdwan years I went from dead last in sales to top man.

I tripled my sales the last two years, and opened some new sales uses for the company product that hadn't been thought of before.

In addition, I believe that for good sales it's important to lay a sound base, and as a result I have been extremely active in community affairs and have many friends and contacts.

My experience I believe fits right in with your needs. Please let me know when we can get together and talk.

This letter adds a lot of enthusiasm and brings out your good points. It hooks in well, has good organization, utilizes some of the motivation factors. This is a better selling letter than the other two, but can be strengthened by adding more of what you can do for the company (other person's needs). Let's do it once more, adding brashness:

---

(4)

Don't do anything until you talk to me.

I know that sounds presumptuous, but I mean it.

I have spent considerable time recently in learning something about your company and I feel your needs and my experience go together well.

I've been in sales 15 years, the last five with Doman Holdwan as senior salesman. During that time I was faced with many of the sales problems your company now seems to have.

And in the face of this I managed to triple sales.

Let's talk and I'll explain further why I think I can do a good job for you.

The differences in these primarily is one of motivation. The better ones here begin to talk about the employer's needs rather than simply stating the qualifications. Good letters answering help wanted ads need to show the employer how the potential employee can help him—briefly.

Brashness is used when there is a good reason to try to attract the added attention, i.e., there is a lot of competition, you have little chance of getting an appointment with a traditional letter, etc.

MEMOS

(1)

In order to eliminate the possibility of overlapping time schedules through related assignments of similar job categories at similar time intervals, each department should set up a separate schedule for each person, showing his authorized assignment, and supervisors should make a daily check to see that all personnel are properly distributed with confirmation of this being submitted to the accounting department personnel.

Now let's examine this memo.

From Figures 1 and 2 we establish the Audience type as *Semiformal,* and the need type as *Semi-Need.*

Here's how it rates:

	Memo Rating			
	Word power element ratings for a Semi-formal audience and a Semi-Need type taken from the Utilization Guide (Figure 3)	Rating of Memo and Revisions on the Communication Elements Rating Scale (Figure 4)		
Plain talk		(1)	(2)	(3)
Readability index	3–5	0	3	3
Conversational tone	3–5	0	3	3
Comes to the point	3–5	4	5	5
Tight writing	5	0	5	5
Commands attention				
Ho-hum crasher	3	2	3	5
Attention getting elements	0–5			
Goals				
Organization				
Logical	3–5	5	5	5
Impact formula				
Image projection	3–5	0	3	3
Emotion				
Emotional goal	3–5	3	3	3
Earns appeals	0	2	2	5
Motivation				
Future promise	0–3	0	0	5
"I factor"	0–5	3	5	5
Other person's needs	2	3	3	5
Brashness				
		22	40	52

Memos actually have two purposes. The need type in a memo can be either *Semi-Need* where it's necessary to establish *why,* or straight *communication.* If you have some need to explain to get cooperation then it will be *Semi-Need.* The audience type is usually *Semiformal.* This first memo needs to establish a need. It should have a readability index of 3 (Figure 3), have fair conversational tone, come to the point well, be tight, start with a partial ho-hum crasher, use good attention getting elements, be logical, and contain some good basic words for image projection.

These elements need correcting:

readability index
conversational tone
coming to the point
tight writing
better attention getting elements
better explanation (other person's needs)

The first memo is extremely unwieldy and has so many extra words it's difficult to handle. This one problem alone can make the memo extremely ineffective. First let's simply correct the two elements of readability index and conversational tone.

(2)

To keep from having two people working the same job at the same time, departments should have an assignment sheet and schedule for each person. They should then check daily to make sure each worker is on the right job. This confirmation is then to be sent on to the accounting department.

Now let's fix the other elements, giving a good explanation and adding some good attention getting elements.

(3)

This memo is important:

Recently we have had a number of cases in which two people were assigned the same job. And in one case two employees actually sat around all day while the third did all the work.

This is costly and inefficient.

To correct it please do the following:

    1. Please make up a work schedule daily for each man.
    2. Check each worker daily.
    3. Send a confirmation to the accounting department.

For a very short memo such as this is it's best to simply say it and get it over with. It has good goals, it's organized well, it has a little image projection in that instead of saying "submitted to the accounting department" the writer says "sent." "Instead of overlapping time schedules," he says, "working the same job," so there is some visualization here. There is no emotional goal, no appeals, no future promise, no "I factor," no other person's needs. For a short memo, however, the second does a pretty good job and it scores 31 points.

PAMPHLETS

Pamphlets can be either third person or second, and they both need to establish a need and do some selling in most cases. The audience type is *Semiformal* and *Conversational.* Here's one:

Our camp program was modified to take all factors into consideration without exception, so it will promote maximum growth for each of the individuals by considering each need separately.

This particular pamphlet has a *Need to Sell* and it should be *Conversational* (Figures 1 and 2).

As you can see the first one has few of the word power elements. Pamphlets like this (see Utilization Chart) need to use good image projection techniques, examples and word pictures.

In addition all word power elements need correcting. In the first revision we'll fix the readability index, add a conversational tone and give it more image projection.

Revision (1)

After reviewing last year's camp program we decided to change our six basic program areas—swimming, archery, horseback riding, hiking, camping, and boating—and add one more—nature study. Since we feel that a camper does much better in areas that he is interested in, we are going first to give him a brief smattering of each area. Then we will encourage him to choose one or two to explore. If he's interested in swimming, for instance, he can swim up to three hours a day, and receive advanced instruction. If it's nature, we will encourage him to undertake some nature project. By stressing this approach in all areas we will be able to help each camper get the most out of his camp program.

THE RATINGS FOR THE THREE PAMPHLETS

	Word power element ratings for a *Converational* audience & a *Need to sell* need type taken from the Utilization Guide (Figure 3)	Rating of phamplet & revisions on the Communications Elements Rating Scale (Figure 4)		
		Original	Revisions (1)	(2)
Plain talk				
Readability index	5	0	4	4
Conversational tone	5	0	4	4
Comes to the point	3-5	5	5	5
Tight writing	5	5	4	4
Commands attention				
Ho-hum crasher	3-5	0	1	4
Attention getting elements	3	2	2	2
Goals	3-5	5	5	5
Organization				
Logical	3-5	5	5	5
Impact formula				
Image projection	3-5	0	4	4
Emotion				
Emotional goal	3-5	2	5	5
Earns appeals	3-5	0	3	5
Motivation				
Future promise	3-5	3	5	5
"I factor"	3-5	0	0	5
Other person's needs	3-5	0	0	5
Brashness	—	—	—	—
		27	47	62

Now let's add the other person's needs. The final version helps add appeals to it by talking directly to the reader about something he's really interested in—his own son's welfare.

Revision (2)

We know you want your son to get as much out of his summer as possible. For this reason, we have decided to change our six basic program areas—swimming, archery, horseback riding, hiking, camping, and boating—and add one more—nature study. Since we feel that a camper does much better in areas he's interested in, we've changed our approach to give a brief smattering of each area, then we encourage him to choose one or two to explore in more depth.

If he's interested in swimming, for instance, he can swim up to three hours a day and receive considerable advanced instruction. If it's nature, we will encourage him to undertake some nature project. By stressing this approach in all areas, we believe we will be able to help your son get the most out of his camp program.

Since this is in the third person you should concentrate mainly on the communication elements and include good attention getting elements and a good explanation.

REPORTS

Structural Visualization and School Troubles

Mature men, with authority and responsibilities, but high in structural visualization, too often resign impulsively to their own disadvantage after ten or 12 years at an executive desk, while others, low in the same trait, gradually take over the administration and control. Exhorting the high structure men to persist, to concentrate, to form good work habits is not the answer. They fail to find in desk work the happiness they anticipated from life.

How, then, can education expect boys, new to the world, possessing the same structural trait, and with no experience of satisfying achievements on which to build sustaining confidence in themselves and their judgment, to sit with any sense of enjoyment 12 to 15 years at a school desk?

Though every unused aptitude leads to uneasiness, a dissatisfaction with one's self and one's accomplishments, why should structural visualization, so valuable in the modern world, cause school trouble, foment restlessness when idle, more seemingly than any other characteristic? From first grade, accounting aptitude plays a daily part in school, and is used unconsciously. Creative imagination, ideaphoria, leads one's fancies, though not always constructively. Tonal memory, the music aptitude, finds outlet. Laboratory biology taxes structural visualization, but the subject is too often a lecture course. Not until physics, offered in the last year before college, do schools give an opportunity for the expression of this structural trait. Structurally minded boys feel instinctively they possess something, but endure 11 years of schooling without recognition, and even in physics, awaited impatiently, a boy may encounter a non-structural teacher, for as a group, educators average low in structural visualization.

Most reports should *Establish A Need* and be *Semiformal* (Figures 1 and 2).

Check its rating on page 204.

This report is typical but bad. It has a readability index of 0, it is not conversational, it fails to come to the point. It rambles, it is not very logical, and it has no image projection.

Here's what we need to correct:

readability index
conversational tone
coming to the point
tight writing
organization
image projection—examples etc.

The Revision

Children with high structural visualization often have trouble in school and many times actually hate it. The reason is that children with these traits want desperately to use them, yet there is little possibility in most schools. Other traits are used: accounting aptitude, creative imagination, tonal memory, music aptitude, and others. But high structural visualization has little outlet.

Some structural visualization can be used in biological laboratory, but this often is a lecture course. And in most schools it is not until the last year or two when the students take physics that they are allowed to use structural visualization to any degree. Even here they may run up against a non-structural teacher who keeps the opportunities to use this trait at a minimum.

In one classroom, for instance, the teacher who rated low in structural visualization gave the students experiments to perform, yet never gave the students any time to do them. Day after day he simply talked throughout the lab period and at the end told them to put their materials away.

Is it any surprise, then, that children with high structural visualization often are impatient and get extremely discouraged? They recognize that they have an unused ability, but because educators as a group average low in structural visualization, and school simply isn't set up that way, they simply have no outlet.

The same problem, of course, occurs in adult life. Mature men, high in structural visualization who have authority and responsibility yet aren't using this trait as much as they like, often simply give up while others low in this trait take over. As a result we often find men with tremendous ability who simply haven't achieved their potential.

Since this report needs to explain the points effectively, it should make some use of image projection as it does. The report now is readable, makes its points effective, and is easy to understand.

IN CONCLUSION

Thus, Word Power Dynamics is the science of effective communications combined with motivational psychology to make writing produce results. It is, as you know, unique, different, and extremely effective. And if you are a typical reader, it has already revolutionized your writing methods.

In addition, as you continue to polish your word power tools through use, you will soon find that you will be able to produce action from your writing that not only seems miraculous but which at one time you would have considered almost impossible to achieve.

	Word Power element ratings for a semi-fromal audience & an establish a need need type taken from the Utilization Guide (Figure 3).	Rating of this report & the revisions on the Communications Elements Rating Scale (Figure 4).	
		Report	Revision
Plain Talk			
Readability index	5	0	3
Conversational tone	5	0	3
Come to the point	3–5	2	5
Tight writing	5	0	5
Commands attention			
Ho-hum crasher	3–5	1	2
Attention getting			
elements	3	0	—
Goals	3–5	4	4
Organization			
Logical	3–5	2	5
Impact formula			
Image projection	3–5	—	5
Emotion			
Emotional goal	3–5	5	5
Earns appeals	0–3	2	2
Motivation			
Future promise	3	—	1
"I factor"	0–5*	0	—
Other person's needs	2–4	0	—
Brashness			
		16	40

*See Utilization Guide explanation.